AFRICA IN THE MODERN WORLD

General Editor GWENDOLEN M. CARTER

L I B E R I A

The Evolution of
Privilege

J. GUS LIEBENOW

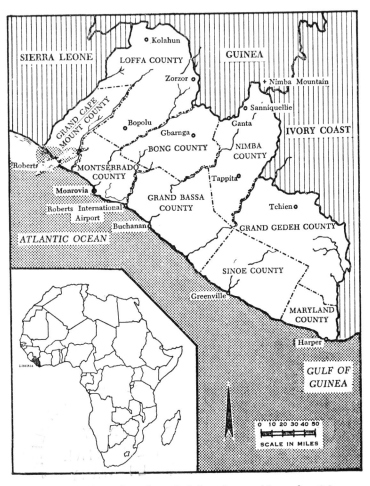

Liberia (following the administrative revision of 1964)

LIBERIA

The Evolution of Privilege

J. GUS LIEBENOW

INDIANA UNIVERSITY

Cornell University Press

ITHACA AND LONDON

Standard Book Number 8014–0506–8

Library of Congress Catalog Card Number 69–18359

PRINTED IN THE UNITED STATES OF AMERICA
BY THE VAIL-BALLOU PRESS, INC.

Foreword

No country in Africa has a stronger claim on American interest than Liberia. Its long-entrenched ruling group—the Americo-Liberians—came originally from the United States or from ships forced by the United States navy to release their slaves. The organizing group that founded Liberia in 1822—the American Colonization Society—included such prominent Americans as President James Monroe and General Andrew Jackson. Initially, though never wholeheartedly, the American federal government was persuaded to make a series of grants for land, homes, equipment, and teachers, and to accept the Society's agent in West Africa as its own. The increasing indifference of the American government helped to spur Liberia's declaration of independence in 1847, but there have always been strong informal ties between the two countries, particularly through the efforts of voluntary societies.

At a time when black separatism in the United States is becoming more pronounced, the progress in Africa of a black-governed state with this background has particular importance. That the story is disturbing makes it no less important. Americo-Liberians, particularly of the governing class, have long sought, with signal success, to capitalize on their privileged social and economic position. Pioneers of a one-party state in Africa, using unchallengeable political control to secure rich material rewards, the Amer-

v

ico-Liberian elite has maintained its often oppressive domination over the majority tribal people and exploited its
own poorer groups. In a curious contrast to the process in
other independent African states, Liberia's ruling minority has deliberately depended on foreigners for economic
skills and development. The country's elite controls impressive natural resources but—as the most trenchant
analysis of Liberia's economic system, *Growth without
Development,* points out—it has not noticeably improved
the standard of living of the great majority of Liberians or
prepared them for significant roles in their expanding
economy.[1]

What is surprising in the face of such a situation is that
Liberia and, in particular, its redoubtable President, William S. Tubman, have established positions that are so
apparently secure and respected among the newer independent African-controlled states, all of which hold aspirations and pursue policies much more liberal and populist
in character. In part this reaction is because Tubman's
version of Pan-Africanism—which the author defines as
gradualism, economic and cultural cooperation as precursor to political discussion, and regional rather than
continental cooperation—has appealed more to them than
did Nkrumah's blueprint for continental political unity.
In part it is a tribute to Tubman's diplomatic skills and his
willingness to identify so fully with opposition to discrimi-
natory white minority regimes in southern Africa.

Whether or not approved external policies can compensate in the eyes of other African-controlled countries for a

[1] Robert W. Clower, George Dalton, Mitchell Harwitz, and A. A.
Walters, *Growth without Development: An Economic Survey of
Liberia* (Evanston: Northwestern Univ. Press, 1966).

restrictive system at home, it is hard to imagine that the latter can long survive the Tubman regime. As in other states, like Ethiopia, that are heavily dependent for cohesion and character on a single dominant person, Liberia's future after Tubman retires or dies is a topic of constant speculation. Can the country make the transition peacefully to a more equalitarian society? Will there be a radical change in the base of political power and the direction of policies? Will the military prove the next ruling group? If so, will it introduce reforms or merely reinforce the existing structure of society and politics? All that can safely be anticipated is change, but in African states this has more often been in form rather than in basic characteristics. So one is left with the question posed by the author: "After Tubman, what?"

GWENDOLEN M. CARTER

Northwestern University
April 1969

Acknowledgments

The enthusiastic response of a number of young Liberians to my various writings on West Africa's oldest republic had convinced me that a book on the politics of Liberia was long overdue. Thus, I welcomed the suggestion to prepare a volume on Liberia to be included by Cornell University Press in its new series "Africa in the Modern World."

A field trip to Liberia and Sierra Leone in 1960–1961 and subsequent visits to West Africa in 1965 and 1967 provided the basic data for this book. The initial research was made possible by a fifteen-month grant from the Social Science Research Council to carry out a comparative study of the development of political and administrative leadership in Liberia and Sierra Leone. I became so fascinated with the inner dynamics of the Liberian political system—largely ignored by other scholars—that I devoted the greater portion of my time to that country. My briefer stay in Sierra Leone provided comparative data and enabled me to pursue clues to the understanding of Liberia's historical and familial ties and to examine archival materials obtainable only in Freetown or on the Sierra Leone side of the border.

Gradually, as the intricate web of politics in this modern-day version of a Renaissance Italian city-state unfolded, I became convinced that an analysis of Liberian society could contribute much to our understanding both of situations of colonial rule and of the processes of modernization in aristocratic societies. There were many similarities, for example, between my previous studies of British colonial administration in Tanganyika and my observations of the methods employed by the Americo-Liberian minority in controlling the tribal people in the Liberian hinterland. I felt, too, that my studies on Liberian modernization complemented those being done by European and American scholars in Ethiopia, Burundi, and other sectors of the African continent. I was especially pleased, for example, to receive a letter in 1963 from Michael Lofchie at the conclusion of his stay in prerevolutionary Zanzibar, noting the similarities between the processes of modernization in that Arab-dominated dependency in East Africa and the situation I had described in West Africa.

Liberia is a complex country, and various visitors have had various experiences in one region or another of the country that have led them to differing interpretations of the pace and direction of change. My own thesis, I believe, is historically correct; it has received wide support by Liberian and foreign scholars alike. Parenthetically, it is a tribute to the Liberian elite and to President Tubman personally that a study such as mine, which may seem critical of them, could have been conducted. Indeed, there have been many healthy signs indicating that Liberia is becoming even more receptive to research on a wide range of subjects, and there is a growing spirit of cooperation between Liberian and foreign scholars.

For permission to use portions of my previous articles on Liberia which appeared in *African One-Party States,* edited by Gwendolen M. Carter (Cornell University Press, 1962), and in *Political Parties and National Integration in*

Tropical Africa, edited by James Coleman and Carl G. Rosberg (University of California Press, 1964), I want to express my appreciation to the publishers. I also acknowledge the permission granted by Northwestern University Press to use several tables and to quote from *Growth without Development: An Economic Survey of Liberia* (1966) by Robert W. Clower, George Dalton, Mitchell Harwitz, and A. A. Walters.

Although there are many Liberians as well as American expatriates resident in Liberia whose assistance I would like to acknowledge, I have refrained from doing so in order to accept full responsibility myself for the various interpretations and conclusions here presented. I would, however, like to express the sincere gratitude of myself and my family for the friendship and hospitality afforded us by Mary and George, Sam and Bertha, George and Vivian, Dora, and the late Bishop and Albert. Above all, however, I want to express my deepest thanks to Beverly, for her constant encouragement, her very helpful criticism of this and previous writings, her resourcefulness in the construction of the political genealogy, and especially for her patience. It is to her and my children that I dedicate this book.

J. GUS LIEBENOW

Bloomington, Indiana
November 1968

Contents

Introduction

The primary African concern with dislodging European
minorities from their positions of privilege in areas south
of the Sahara has tended to focus attention during the past
two decades upon only one kind of imperialism. In fact,
the European subjugation of Africa has been merely one
of the more recent—and more pervasive—instances of imperialism that have plagued the people of that continent
during countless centuries. Even the Arab incursions in
northern and eastern regions during the five hundred
years prior to the European arrival were themselves pre-
ceded by the establishment of large-scale empire-kingdoms
throughout the western Sudanic area. For the most part
these imperial expansions found Africans subordinating
other Africans for the purposes of political, economic, and
religious exploitation.

Even during the Western European conquest of Africa
during the latter half of the nineteenth century, the British, French, German, and other colonialists found themselves in competition with African military groups who
were also attempting to superimpose their hegemony over
large quarters of the continent. In the west, for example,
French imperial designs were temporarily thwarted by the
religiously inspired followers of the Muslim leader Sam-
ory, and by the successors to El Hadj Omar in their conquest of land and souls across the entire West African
savanna. In their penetration of eastern Africa, the British

found a willing ally in the Ganda, who were themselves in the process of establishing control over the Nyoro, Toro, and other tribes northwest of Lake Victoria. An even more dramatic case of competition between European and African imperialisms occurred in the southern and eastern regions of the continent. There, the Afrikaner, British, German, and Portuguese expansionists found themselves challenged by one of the most remarkable military movements in the history of Africa. Following the Zulu-Ngoni military diaspora, emanating from southern Africa during the 1820's, Ngoni raiding parties within the next half century founded new communities as far north as Lake Victoria and continually terrorized scores of tribal groups in the intervening area.

In addition to direct European conquest and colonization in Africa, there were instances of imperialism at the end of the eighteenth and the turn of the nineteenth centuries that were "Western" in inspiration but were promoted by persons who had been excluded from full participation in Western society. One of the earliest of these enterprises was the founding of Freetown in Sierra Leone in 1787. Most of the initial settlers at Freetown were former Negro slaves freed by the first "emancipation proclamation" in North America—the promise of Sir Henry Clinton, the British commanding general in the South during the American Revolution, to guarantee the freedom of all slaves who deserted their rebellious masters.[1] Eventually many of these freed slaves found their way to West Africa by way of Nova Scotia or Britain. Once "repatriated" to

[1] F. A. J. Utting, *The Story of Sierra Leone* (London: Longmans, 1931), pp. 31–35.

Africa, the former slaves, who eventually came to be known as Creoles, gradually took on all the attitudes of an alien settler community in their relations with the indigenous Africans. Only the continued presence of British colonial officers—many of whom resented the Creoles and wanted to avoid interethnic conflict between the settlers and the chiefs of the interior—prevented the Creoles from dominating the tribal people. When Sierra Leone attained independence in 1961, the government was controlled by persons whose antecedents were tribal rather than Creole.

The second major experiment in the "repatriation" of freed Negroes and persons of mixed ancestry was the founding of Liberia in 1822. Despite initial American involvement, no colonial officers remained in a supervisory capacity beyond the tutelary period. In 1847 the settlers declared Liberia an independent republic. Although a century later descendants of the early settlers were lamenting that they had not "reaped the advantages of colonialism," they had nevertheless managed to create between themselves and the indigenous tribal people a relationship that President William V. S. Tubman in 1960 labeled colonial in character.[2] A colonial, or dependency, situation is defined as any case in which the authoritative allocation of values for one fairly distinct society or several combined societies is performed in large measure by individuals and

[2] Most frequently quoted in this regard are the remarks made by Liberia's Ambassador Charles King at the United Nations during the celebration of Ghana's independence in 1957. King was the son of a former President of Liberia. See *New York Times,* 24 March 1957.

The remarks of President Tubman were made during his first Annual Message to the 44th Legislature of Liberia, 22 Nov. 1960.

groups representing a second distinct society.[3] Thus, the superior group in the relationship monopolizes the use of force, establishes the primary goals for all societies concerned, limits the means for attaining these goals, and attempts to determine the ultimate outcome of the relationship—continued domination, a form of integration, or eventual separation of the several societies. The relationship of the Americo-Liberians to the tribal peoples of Liberia fits this definition.

Since 1822 the Americo-Liberian settlers and their descendants have become masters of the art of survival in a potentially hostile world. On many occasions in the past the very existence of the Republic was threatened either by an armed uprising on the part of the conquered tribal people or by the diplomatic and other victories of their colonial neighbors, the British and the French. Although the tribal threat to Americo-Liberian supremacy has persisted, the European colonial threat has been replaced by the potentially greater dangers posed by the ideologies of Liberia's independent neighbors: Sierra Leone, the Ivory Coast, and, particularly, Guinea. Official apprehensiveness regarding Liberia's own well-being in an independent Africa was clearly stated by its Secretary of Defense in his *Annual Report for 1960:*

With the attainment of independence of our sister African brothers contiguous to our borderline, problems which we never thought of are arising and have to be grappled with every degree of efficiency and alertness. Not only are the problems of the crossing into our territories of citizens of other

[3] For a fuller explanation see my article "Legitimacy of Alien Relationship: The Nyaturu of Tanganyika," *Western Political Quarterly,* XIV (March 1961), 64–86.

states involved but also the question of national ideologies, some of which are divergent to ours and destined to threaten and uproot the very foundation upon which our democratic institution was founded. To ensure that the situation just referred to will be averted and not permitted to take a foothold in Liberia we have to strengthen and increase our border control units and give more attention to border problems as they arise from day to day.

That the Americo-Liberian leadership has been able to withstand this modern challenge to its authority is due in large measure to the political adroitness of President William V. S. Tubman, who has governed Liberia since New Year's Day, 1944. Before Tubman assumed office, Liberia was frequently despised by the emergent nationalist elite of other African territories and often cited as an example of extreme underdevelopment. Tubman, after a quarter of a century of rule, has made Liberia one of the leaders in the African bloc in the United Nations. Liberia, moreover, has undergone a rate of economic growth comparable to that experienced in recent years by Japan and other highly developed societies.

World prestige and remarkable economic growth, however, have not brought substantial change in the lives of the tribal people who constitute the bulk of Liberia's million inhabitants.[4] The dominant political minority, the

[4] The 1962 census—the first for the country as a whole—placed the population at 1,016,443. The results were suppressed for four years since they undermined Liberia's usual claim of two million inhabitants. (One official publication put the figure at 3,500,000.) The census also showed an embarrassing discrimination against the tribal majority of the hinterland in terms of political representation and distribution of economic benefits.

Americo-Liberians, are estimated at less than 10 per cent of the total population. By various mechanisms, for a century and a half they have not only dominated the political destinies of the tribal majority but also controlled the evolution of most economic, educational, social, and religious structures within the Republic. Although outwardly much has changed in the "new" Liberia, the essentially aristocratic relationship between the descendants of the settlers and the descendants of the original tribal inhabitants has remained substantially the same. The most significant difference is that privilege has been raised to a new level of magnitude.

LIBERIA

The Evolution of
Privilege

CHAPTER 1

The Tree of Liberty
Bears Bitter Fruit

The founding of Liberia was inspired by a number of prominent white Americans concerned with slavery, the slave trade, and the untenable position of "free persons of color" in the United States following the formation of the Federal Republic in 1787. Emigration or repatriation to Africa, however, was not the only solution offered. Indeed, Thomas Jefferson in 1784, Governor James Monroe of Virginia in 1801, and James Forten as well as other free Negroes of the Philadelphia Bethel Church in 1816 were among those who advocated various plans to establish "black states" or territories in Louisiana, along the Missouri River, in the Pacific Northwest, or at other places in North America.[1] Ultimately the leaders of the colonization movement decided that the only feasible solution was to establish a colony on the West Coast of Africa to serve as a refuge for freed American Negroes who desired repatriation to the land of their ancestors. The white founders

---

[1] One of the more interesting historical studies of the efforts to colonize Liberia is contained in P. J. Staudenraus, *The African Colonization Movement, 1816–1865* (New York: Columbia University Press, 1961). The standard work on the legal, constitutional, and historical background of the colonial period is Charles H. Huberich, *The Political and Legislative History of Liberia*, 2 vols. (New York: Central Book Co., 1947).

felt that this could also provide an answer to the embarrassing question of what to do with the Ibos, Dahomeans,
Congolese, and other Africans taken from slaving vessels
intercepted by the United States navy following the ban
on importation of slaves after 1808 and the agreement of
1819 to help suppress the slave trade on the high seas.

The American Heritage

The motivations of those who organized the American
Colonization Society in 1816 were decidedly mixed. Some
saw emigration as a convenient device for ridding cities
both north and south of a class that had only a vague legal
status and was regarded as a constant source of social fric-
tion. Indeed, the concern of these pragmatists mounted as
the ranks of the free Negroes grew from roughly eighty
thousand in 1790 to over twice that number three decades
later.[2] The Southern planters, who figured prominently in
the resettlement movement, were even more vitally interested in eliminating a class whose very existence constituted an economic and political threat to the institution of
slavery. Other supporters of the Colonization Society, such
as Robert Finley, a Presbyterian minister from New Jer-
sey, William Thornton, a leading Quaker from New York,
John Caldwell of the American Bible Society, and a host of
Baptist, Congregationalist, and other Protestant spokes-
men, saw the colony of American Negroes as a beachhead
for Christianity and Western civilization, spreading the
Gospel—as well as pacificism, prohibition, and other ex-
periments in morality—to Africa. Finally, others, moved by
more secular humanitarian considerations, took the position that the free Negroes were capable of improvement

[2] Huberich, *op. cit.*, I, 45.

and self-government but that the entrenched prejudice of the white community and the belief of the Negroes in their own inferiority made it impossible for them to compete on equal terms in a mixed society.[3] Thus, by the humanitarian standards of that age, repatriation provided a morally just solution to the racial situation.

Whatever the motives of the American founders of Liberia, there was little doubt about their ability ultimately to translate their interest into political reality. Their membership included not only influential Protestant clergy but also a cadre of some of the most prominent names in American politics. The officers and sympathetic supporters of the American Colonization Society included Supreme Court Justice Bushrod Washington, nephew and heir of the late President, President James Monroe, four subsequent contenders for the presidency (Speaker of the House Henry Clay, General Andrew Jackson, Secretary of the Treasury William Crawford, and Congressman Daniel Webster of New Hampshire), and many prominent private citizens of the Revolutionary and Federalist periods of American history: Francis Scott Key, John Randolph of Roanoke, and John Taylor of Caroline.

Although the American Colonization Society was not entirely successful in its endeavors to have the federal government underwrite the entire scheme, they did get the administration of President James Monroe (for whom the capital of Liberia was later named) to accept the Society's agent in West Africa as its own agent in the suppression of the slave trade and the resettlement of rescued Africans. Of even greater significance was the Society's victory in getting the United States Congress to appropriate $100,000—

[3] Staudenraus, *op. cit.,* pp. 19–22.

the first of a series of grants—to assist in the purchase of land, the construction of homes and forts, the acquisition of farm implements, the payment of teachers, and the carrying out of other projects necessary to the care, training, and defense of the settlers. The U.S. government outfitted the *Elizabeth,* which was accompanied by the U.S.S. *Cyane,* in an attempt in 1820 to settle American Negroes on Sherbro Island, off Sierra Leone. The settlement scheme proved abortive, and in the following year Lieutenant Robert F. Stockton of the U.S. navy rescued Elijah Johnson and other survivors of malaria at Sherbro and carried them, as well as a new group of settlers from America, farther down the coast. The actual landing site of Cape Mesurado, near the present city of Monrovia, was selected by a young lieutenant named Matthew Perry, who later achieved fame as Commodore of the Africa Squadron and in the opening of Japan to Western influence.[4]

The negotiations at Cape Mesurado were protracted and heated. At gunpoint, Lt. Stockton attempted to convince "King Peter" and other minor Bassa and Dey chieftains that the settlers came as benefactors, not enemies. The American officer successfully negotiated the deeding of Cape Mesurado to the Colonization Society in return for $300 worth of muskets, beads, tobacco, gunpowder, clothing, mirrors, food, and rum. This was the first of an endless string of transactions in which the tribal negotiators only belatedly realized the full implication of the "sale" of their land to the alien settlers from America.

The American relationship to its stepchild on the African West Coast has been ambiguous during most of the century and a half since the initial settlement. The U.S.

[4] See Samuel E. Morison, *"Old Bruin," Commodore Matthew C. Perry* (London: Oxford University Press, 1968).

government steadfastly refused to recognize the purchased area as an official colony, which created many international problems for the Colonization Society, the settlers, and the American government itself. This studied official aloofness assumed monumental proportions in the 1840's, when the British government, in support of European traders from Sierra Leone who ignored Liberian land claims and refused to pay customs fees, declined to acknowledge the sovereignty of the American Colonization Society. Although the United States expressed to the British its concern for the rights of the settlers, it was the Americo-Liberians themselves who resolved the impasse. In 1847 their "Declaration of Independence" severed ties with the founding Society and established Liberia as the first sovereign and independent Negro state in Africa.[5] The almost immediate recognition of the new republic by Great Britain contrasts sharply with the American stance. Despite continued economic and military support, it was not until the administration of Abraham Lincoln, in 1862—when the Civil War had removed the principal objectors to the presence of a Negro envoy in Washington, D.C.—that recognition was extended.

A gradual shift to dependence upon the British became very noticeable in the latter decades of the nineteenth century, despite conflict over land claims in the interior. In 1871, for example, the Liberian government turned to the

[5] Similar action was taken by the settlers who had established themselves further down the coast near Cape Palmas. This effort was fostered by the Maryland State Colonization Society, which broke away from the American Colonization Society in 1831 and started sending settlers to Maryland in Liberia in 1833. It remained a separate colony and republic until 1857, when it was annexed by the Republic of Liberia. See Huberich, *op. cit.,* I, II, *passim.*

British for a loan when it found itself in dire financial straits. Unfortunately, the results of this loan were disastrous for the Liberian people, for President Edward J. Roye (who was deposed as a result of having profited personally from the transactions), and indeed for everyone except the London bankers. British-Liberian ties were also manifest in the education of Liberian youth in England and Sierra Leone, in trade relations, and in the financial and other forms of assistance given by the British government in the reorganization of the Republic's administrative services and military forces.

Nonetheless, the American connection remained strong despite the lack of direct assistance from other than missionary sources during the first half century of independence. The United States was, indeed, influential in maintaining the independence of Liberia even if it was not prepared to do more than admonish the British and French when they whittled away Liberia's extended territorial claims in the hinterland. In 1909, for instance, an American commission of inquiry, by its very presence and its recommendations (never officially accepted by the U.S. government), prevented both England and France from taking over the country as a protectorate as a result of Liberia's defaulting on the repayment of a series of European loans.

Liberian fears regarding British intentions were far from groundless. Indeed, the British Governor of Sierra Leone, Sir Leslie Probyn, suggested in a secret letter to the Colonial Office that Britain take over northwestern Liberia because the Sierra Leone Railway lay so close to the Liberian border. "It seems to me," Probyn wrote, "that a country owning a Railway in Africa is the natural overlord or suzerain of the country situated within say 50 miles of the Railway." He proposed that Britain "lease" Liberian territory along the lines of the leaseholds by the European powers in China. His chief desire, he insisted, was "that some method should be found whereby the interior of that part of Liberia which is adjacent to [Sierra Leone] can be properly governed." [6]

American diplomatic concern was also useful during World War I. In 1915 the United States forestalled British intervention in Liberia during an uprising on the Kru Coast by providing the Americo-Liberians with arms and military advisers to help crush the tribal rebellion. Fifteen years later, however, the American relationship once more took on an ambiguous quality during the League of Nations investigation of slavery and contract labor in Liberia. Details of the League inquiry are discussed in Chapter 4; suffice it to note at this point that although the American association with the League inquiry offended many Liberian officials, the United States action was instrumental in frustrating the efforts of the European powers to place Liberia under some form of international control.[7] From the early 1930's onward the relations between the United States and Liberia have steadily improved in the fields of economic development (Chapter 9) and foreign affairs (Chapter 10).

[6] Sierra Leone Archives. Confidential letter of Governor Probyn to Lord Elgin, 28 March 1906. Letter box, no reference number.

[7] For a good treatment of the subject, see the unpublished article by Wolfe W. Schmokel, "Reform and Rubber: The United States and the Crisis of Liberian Independence, 1929–1934," University of Vermont, 1963.

The Condition and Aspirations of the Settlers

Despite the enthusiasm of the white founders of the American Colonization Society, the efforts at emigration or repatriation had affected only a small fraction of the free Negroes and mulattoes, whose number had risen to a quarter of a million by 1867. The figures in Table 1 indicate that less that twenty thousand persons were settled in Liberia, and close to six thousand of these had never been to America, for they were Africans rescued or "recaptured," from slaving vessels on the high seas.

Table 1. Status of Liberian immigrants, 1822–1867

Born free	4,541
Purchased their freedom	344
Emancipated to go to Liberia	5,957
Emancipated for other reasons	753
Arrived from Barbados, 1865	346
Unknown	68
Settled in Maryland County, 1831–1862, origins not indicated	1,227
Recaptured Africans sent by the United States navy	5,722
Total	18,958

Adapted from Merran Fraenkel, *Tribe and Class in Monrovia* (Oxford Univ. Press, 1964), p. 6.

The limited success of the colonization scheme was in part due to finances. The Society failed to get the U.S. government to underwrite the operation, and few liberated Negroes possessed the property necessary to pay their own way to Liberia as well as survive the first harvest. The emigrants were thus dependent upon funds provided by former masters who had emancipated their slaves, the appropriations by various state legislatures in America, and the private fund-raising ability of the Society. There were other reasons, however, for the poor showing. The abolitionists and antislavery people, for example, felt that repatriation actually undermined their case since it removed from American shores the evidence that free Negroes could be industrious and gave support to the notion that the two races could not exist in peace within a single society. This objection was voiced by many freed Negroes as well; the leaders of the Philadelphia Bethel Church in 1816 labeled the colonization scheme a slur upon their reputation and little more than a plan to dump free Negroes "into the savage wilds of Africa." It was, they claimed, "a circuitous route" back to bondage.[8]

The aspirations of the settlers—or Americo-Liberians, as they eventually came to be called—were mixed. The core of dynamic leadership during the formative years were the five thousand immigrants who had been born free or who had been sufficiently enterprising in America to purchase their freedom. The ambitions of many in this group paralleled those of the white founders of the Society. Men like Lott Carey and Colin Teague, who were Baptist preachers, not only tended to the needs of the settlers but carried the Gospel as well to the tribal people along the coast. As Carey, a former warehouse hand from Richmond, Virginia, said: "I am an African. I wish to go to a country where I shall be estimated by my merits, not by my complexion; and I feel bound to labour for my suffering race." [9] So enterprising were Negro and white missionaries

[8] Staudenraus, *op. cit.,* p. 32.
[9] *Ibid.,* p. 109.

alike that by 1838 there were over twenty churches along the coast representing most of the major Protestant denominations.[10]

The church became a vital social institution to the settler in building new bonds in a strange land. Churches have borne (and continue to bear) the major educational burden in Liberia. By 1838 there were ten schools founded by church groups and staffed in most cases by Negro settlers; the teaching profession was one of the few white-collar positions open to free Negroes in the pre-Civil War South. The churches were equally important in launching newspapers in the colony, and the four presses in the early years were crucial in providing information on new crops, ship arrivals, market conditions, and other data about the environment. Later, several of the church presses became important political instruments. One editor, the Reverend John Seys, used his newspaper to supplement his pulpit criticism of the American Colonization Society and its administration of the colony.

Without the enthusiastic cooperation between the better educated settlers and the white leaders who came out as the agents or governors in behalf of the American Colonization Society, the experiment in repatriation would have failed. A remarkable sense of dedication on the part of the

[10] Methodists, Baptists, Congregationalists, Episcopalians, and Presbyterians dominated at the outset. The Lutherans, who are strong today, did not arrive until the American Civil War. The various Pentacostal groups, who now rank second only to the Methodists, did not appear until the beginning of the twentieth century. The Roman Catholics had a late start in the last quarter of the nineteenth century but had to abandon their mission temporarily before resuming work in earnest in Maryland and Montserrado counties in 1906.

white leaders was demonstrated by the first agents—Dr. Eli Ayres, a surgeon from Baltimore, and Jehudi Ashmun, a young Methodist minister—through the last white administrator, Governor Thomas Buchanan (brother of the future President of the United States), who died at his post in 1841. Despite the periods of crisis, the agents had generally high praise for the courage and endurance of many of the educated Americo-Liberians. Several of the settlers, such as Lott Carey, A. D. Williams, and the very gifted Joseph Jenkins Roberts, had taken over the administration of the Society's affairs during the temporary absences of the white agents from Liberia. Elijah Johnson, a survivor of the ill-fated Sierra Leone landing of 1820, had been the primary organizer of the defense of the settlements near Monrovia. Other Americo-Liberians had surveyed the farm plots and laid out the streets in the infant colony.

While cooperative in most instances, the settlers were far from subservient. They realized all too well their financial dependence upon the Society and their reliance upon the military support of the U.S. navy in resisting tribal and European threats to the life of the colony. Most of this group, however, had come to Liberia to escape white domination. Despite their vague legal status and lack of political influence, many—especially the offspring of illicit unions between slave women and white "gentlemen"—had received quality education, owned a certain amount of property, and even enjoyed a measure of social status. This group was restive under the tight reins of the Society's agents, and they occasionally rebelled. Even the quiet Jehudi Ashmun was forced to move temporarily to the Cape Verde Islands in the face of a revolt organized by Lott Carey.

Particularly annoying to the educated Americo-Liberian were the Jeffersonian ideals of many of the religious and philanthropical supporters of the Society who believed that the independent settlers should seek the serenity of a rural, agricultural existence and disavow the evils of commerce and industry. Despite their origins in the rural South, many of the educated settlers had spent their adult years in the cities of the north or the border states. They associated agriculture with the life of servitude they or their parents had experienced. They did not, moreover, adjust well to the diet of cassava, plantain, yams, and other foods to which Africans were accustomed and preferred the more costly imported maize, wheat flour, pork, and ham, purchased with the profits from petty trading. The educated Americo-Liberian would only associate himself with agriculture as the absentee landlord of a plantation of sugar cane, rice, or coffee cultivated by poorer settlers or African recaptives rescued from slave ships en route to the New World. The role of dirt farmer was decidedly beneath his station.[11]

The disdain for agriculture, unfortunately, also spread to the second strata of Americo-Liberian society, the Negroes who had been emancipated with the express understanding that they go to Liberia. This group lacked the independent means of many in the upper strata, and being generally "pure" Negroes rather than "bright-skinned" mulattoes, they tended to be looked down upon during the early decades of colonial history. Many had been house-

[11] The early agricultural and commercial developments of the colony and Republic are very well described in George W. Brown, *The Economic History of Liberia* (Washington: Assoc. Publishers, Inc., 1941), *passim.*

hold retainers or skilled artisans and were not used to the strenuous life of farming. Even those who had been farm managers or field hands, however, had assumed optimistically that a new life in Africa would hold forth something more than the hard calluses and sweaty brows of the past. Ironically, those compelled to till the soil in order to survive found farming in Liberia more difficult than in America. The torrential rain, which averages over 180 inches between April and October, often washed out the crops that had been planted using techniques developed in a more temperate zone. The rapidly leaching soils and the multitude of crop pests were unfamiliar to the immigrant farmer, and the strength he needed for his heavy chores was often drained by the fever of malaria.

Normally, only those Americo-Liberians who settled some distance from the commercial attractions of Monrovia persevered in agriculture. There were, for example, the band of freemen settled by the Mississippi Colonization Society at the mouth of the Sinoe River in 1838, or the dedicated cluster of Negro Quakers who staked out farms near the mouth of the St. John River in 1835 and whose pacifist beliefs almost led to their total annihilation at the hands of hostile Africans. Curiously, the most successful farmers of all stood at the bottom of the Americo-Liberian social structure. These were the Congo, Dahomean, and Ibo captives who had been taken from slaving vessels and deposited at Monrovia. The captive Africans lacked Western education, were unable to speak either English or the local tribal languages, had been stripped of all their property and family ties, still adhered to their traditional religions and customs, and were entirely dependent on the mercy of the white agents and the Americo-Liberian settlers. Collectively they were referred to as Congoes, a term still current in Liberia. Having been just a few days or perhaps months away from the yam farms in Nigeria or Dahomey, the Congoes were not at all disturbed by the conditions of agriculture in Liberia.

For reasons outlined in subsequent chapters, the preferred vocations of the uppermost strata of Americo-Liberian society today are politics and the law. At the outset of modern Liberian history, however, the prestigious callings were the ministry, teaching, and commerce—with the last assuming increased importance during the first five decades of settlement. Despite the efforts of Ashmun and his successors to place legal and practical restrictions upon trade in favor of agriculture, the Americo-Liberian traders persevered. They gradually displaced the Mandingoes and even the European merchants and monopolized the trade between the coast and the interior. Among tribal persons and Westerners alike the Americo-Liberian trader enjoyed a reputation as a shrewd bargainer who exchanged the cloth, rum, and tobacco from America and Europe for the camwood, cane sugar, palm kernels, rice, and the occasional ivory tusk that tribal traders brought to the coast. Often the enterprising Americo-Liberian trader—at risk to his own life—ventured up the rivers in search of trade items.

Through trade with the interior, by serving as representatives of American and European trading firms, and through investment in the construction of schooners and direct engagement in the transatlantic trade, a number of Americo-Liberians attained substantial wealth. These included Francis Devaney, the former slave of U.S. Speaker of the House Langdon Cheves; Joseph Jenkins Roberts, the first President of Liberia; and Edward Roye, who in 1869 became the first full-blooded Negro to be elected

President of Liberia. By the mid-1870's, however, the Liberian prosperity ended, and the country went into a steady economic decline. A number of factors contributed to the decline, including the worldwide economic depression, the sudden interest of European colonial powers to become more directly involved in the exploitation of Africa, the competition that European steamships provided the Liberian-constructed schooners, the rise of the coffee industry in Brazil and the sugar-beet industry in Europe, and a series of disastrous government loans that wiped out the private fortunes of many public officials involved in the transactions.

Despite the economic decline of the educated fourth of the settler community, they continued to control the political, social, and religious standards of the entire Americo-Liberian group. Their standards were those of the ante bellum American South. Far from rejecting the institutions, values, dress, and speech of a society that had rejected them, the free persons of color painstakingly attempted to reproduce that culture on an alien shore. What they had rejected, apparently, was a situation that denied them full participation in American society. Few, in fact, agreed with Lott Carey in regarding Africa as their home. The experiment in colonization was not the "in-gathering" of Africa's lost children. These were Americans, and their views of Africa and Africans were essentially those of nineteenth-century whites in the United States. The bonds of culture were stronger than the bonds of race, and the settlers clung tenaciously to the subtle differences that set them apart from the tribal "savages" in their midst. It was not then (nor is it today) unusual to hear tribal people refer to the Americo-Liberians as "white" people.

The one American institution modified in the Atlantic

crossing was the family. The extraordinary emphasis that the Americo-Liberian settlers placed upon family ties was undoubtedly a reaction against the cruel and recurrent disruption of the slave family and the status of illegitimacy for the products of mixed unions. The Americo-Liberian has from the outset emphasized family size by combining the bilateralism of the American system (counting kinsmen in both the male and female lines) and the extended character of the African kinship system. Although rejecting the legality of polygamy, the Christian Americo-Liberian has increased his offspring by practicing what this author has referred to as "sequential monogamy," or having only one legal wife at a time. Divorce is a rather simple matter. Moreover, informal unions with Congo women and later with tribal women (for whom traditional bridewealth was paid to relatives) were countenanced. To the credit of the Americo-Liberian mores, illegitimacy is a relatively unknown condition. The "outside children" are invariably given full recognition within the family of the Americo-Liberian father.

In addition to informal liaisons with Congo or tribal women, bright youngsters from these two groupings were fairly early assimilated into the Americo-Liberian family under the "ward" or apprentice system. This situation was legally recognized in 1838. In return for food, clothing, shelter, and often education as well, the ward helped out with the farming and other chores. When the system was abused, it differed little from domestic slavery. In many instances, however, a ward was fully adopted into the Americo-Liberian family and permitted to bear the family name, inherit property, and enjoy the prestige of his "father." However deficient the system might have been, it provided one early avenue for assimilation on the part of Congo and tribal youths.

Expansion into the Interior

In addition to the variety of motives that prompted the white founders and the Americo-Liberians to establish the colony on the West Coast of Africa, it became apparent fairly early that Americo-Liberians themselves believed Liberia had a special meaning for all Africans. Clearly borrowing a page from the contemporary American political scene, President Joseph Jenkins Roberts and other Liberian leaders declared that they had a "Manifest Destiny" to bring civilization to the tribal heathen of the hinterland. Less doctrinaire reasons were advanced to justify the expansion of Liberian influence and control beyond the original settlements at Monrovia, Buchanan, Harper, and other coastal points. Thus, it was argued that the defense and "natural growth" of the colony demanded that the Liberian state expand into the interior.

Americo-Liberian leaders seemed undisturbed by the fact that such expansion would further intensify their minority position within the new state. They were already outnumbered by an indigenous tribal majority having no experience with the New World or Westernized slavery and differing markedly in culture from the immigrant community. Moreover, despite their official motto, "The Love of Liberty Brought Us Here," the Americo-Liberians seemed undisturbed by the fact that the process of expansion created a relationship of political dependency between themselves and the members of more than sixteen tribal groups indigenous to the Liberian hinterland. It was a relationship similar in most respects to that obtaining between whites and Africans in other sectors of the continent. The distinguishing criterion for subordination, however, was not race—though differences in skin pigmentation between the bright-skinned (i.e., persons of mixed ancestry) and dark-skinned Liberians continue to have important social and political consequences even today. Rather, the dependency relationship was based upon differences in culture and upon the barriers erected by the Americo-Liberians against either rapid or widespread assimilation of the dominant culture by the tribal people.

The extension of political control by the Americo-Liberians over the subordinate tribal societies took place over a very long period. In some areas the authority of the settlers and their descendants has been recognized only during the past three to five decades. In many respects this extension followed the pattern established by the French, British, Portuguese, and Afrikaners in enlarging their respective spheres of political influence in Africa. The initial acquisitions of land from the Bassa, Dey, and other coastal chiefs came through the "purchase" by the American Colonization Society of a strip 130 miles long and 40 miles wide in what is now Montserrado County. It was largely through such questionable transactions, moreover, that subsequent strips along the coast and in the river valleys were added between 1821 and 1845—often to forestall French or British incursions into the area. Similarly, much of the disputed area in the Gola and Vai territories later surrendered to the British as a part of Sierra Leone had been claimed by the Americo-Liberians on the basis of purchase. Generally, diplomats in international quarters did not question the legal right of Liberian chiefs to sell land held in communal trust any more than they did the right of chiefs to do so elsewhere in Africa.

An equally effective method of expansion was the establishment of protectorate relationships over certain tribal groups, based upon agreements negotiated between the American Colonization Society (or the successor Liberian government) and tribal chiefs who feared their neighbors more than they did the strangers from America. In many instances the instruments of protection were broadly constructed treaties of friendship, in which the tribal chiefs agreed to end intertribal warfare, submit quarrels to the Liberian government for arbitration, cooperate with the Americo-Liberians in ending the slave trade, and ban certain traditional practices—such as the use of poison ordeals in deciding the question of guilt in a court case. A treaty of this nature was concluded in 1839, for example, following the victory of the Liberian General Joseph Jenkins Roberts over Chief Gatumba of Boporu, or Bopolu. This victory convinced the chiefs in the area northwest of Monrovia that the occasionally inept Liberian military forces could be effective. In other instances tribal groups voluntarily accepted the protection of the Liberian government in the face of threats from neighboring tribes or to avoid French or British domination. In addition to these treaties of friendship and protection, there were many treaties with only limited objectives, such as the development of commerce between the hinterland and Monrovia. Several commercial treaties were negotiated in the 1850's by President Roberts with the Vai, Gola, and Loma tribes. Whether the agreements were broad or limited in scope, however, the settler government rapidly converted the treaties into Liberian deeds of ownership to the territory of the people involved.

The immigrants also emulated their British and French competitors for control of the West Atlantic interior of Af-

rica by considering that journeys of exploration provided
the sponsoring state with a claim to any territory "discov-
ered" by the traveler. Various Liberian presidents commis-
sioned European trading firms to carry out such "journeys
of discovery." Among the most exciting, however, were
several undertaken by Americo-Liberians themselves. The
chronicles of a young Liberian surveyor, Benjamin J. K.
Anderson, who visited the western Mandingo city of Musardu in 1868, rank with some of the best literature in this
genre.[12] Two other Liberians, Seymour and Ash, had earlier explored the area north of the St. Paul River and may
even have reached Nimba Mountain and the headwaters of
the Cavalla River in the northeast. Their purposes were
probably more commercial than political.

Finally, some Americo-Liberian claims to control were
based upon conquest. Many of these military ventures in
the early period against the Dey and Vai were only minor
skirmishes in which the spears and knives of the tribal people proved unequal to the rifles and cannons of the Liberian troops. It was in the defense and expansion of the settler community, however, that some of the early heroes of
Liberian history were created—including Elijah Johnson
(an ancestor of President Tubman's son-in-law) and Ma-
tilda Newport, the Liberian equivalent of the American
Mollie Pitcher. On occasion, however, the natives' superior skill in guerrilla warfare, enhanced by arms secured
from outside sources, tipped the scales temporarily in favor
of the tribal element. In such cases Liberian authority was
established only after many years of fighting and considerable loss of life and property by both sides. The Gola tribe

[12] *Narrative of a Journey to Musardu, the Capital of the Western
Mandingoes* (New York: S. W. Green, 1870).

in the early period and the Grebo and Kru tribes as late as the early decades of the present century are outstanding examples of tribal resistance to Liberian occupation.

Resistance to Expansion

Tribal resistance was not the only source of opposition to Liberian expansion. During the early colonial period Don Pedro Blanco, a mulatto from Brazil, and various European slave traders recognized the obvious threat to their activities posed by the American Colonization Society agents and the settlers, who had the support of the U.S. navy in destroying the various slave factories, or depots, along the coast. Thus, the slave traders openly encouraged the Gola, Bassa, and others to attack the infant Americo-Liberian settlements. Although the combined efforts of the American and British navies eventually eliminated the slave traders, many Americo-Liberian and tribal lives were lost in the process.

Later, as the Americo-Liberians moved inland, they came into conflict with another entrenched element concerned with preserving its commercial interests—the Muslim Mandingoes. The latter had established a fairly high degree of political and religious supremacy over the interior tribes of the West Atlantic region. They had, moreover, effectively monopolized the trade among the tribes of the interior as well as the commerce between Europeans and others at the coast with the tribes of the hinterland. Americo-Liberian merchants were determined to break this Mandingo monopoly, but the military and political organization of this group was much more sophisticated than that of the non-Moslem tribes. Although the Liberians eventually won the struggle for supremacy, lingering animosity has persisted into the present century. The Mandingo are alternately discriminated against and given a favored position relative to the other tribes of the interior. They remain to this day, however, the most significant of the indigenous trading groups in Liberia and travel great distances across the Sahara and throughout West Africa in search of commercial opportunities.

Of another character was the opposition to Liberian expansion raised by the British and the French. The Europeans sometimes accomplished their objectives through outright encouragement of tribal resistance. This was certainly the case in the Kolahun District adjacent to Sierra Leone as late as 1911. More frequently, however, the Europeans won their victories at the conference table. Liberia, with only token or moral support from the United States, often found that the rules for the game of "Partition" changed at the whim of the European players. The British administration in Sierra Leone, for example, would not recognize the authority of the Liberian government to collect customs and otherwise regulate trade in the region west of the Mano River but, on the other hand, held the Liberian government responsible for not protecting the property of British traders against tribal raids in the same region. In the Treaty of 1885, as a result of pressures, the Liberians conceded control of that area to the British. Two decades later the British extended their control over portions of the Kolahun District. Only because of protests from the United States was their seizure limited to a small tract that was "exchanged" for a pocket of forest area east of the Mano River.

While the British were active in the west, the French pressed their claims in the east. In 1892 the French suddenly annexed to the Ivory Coast the fifty-mile stretch of coast between the Cavalla and San Pedro rivers and much of the hinterland as well. Liberian protests were based upon treaties concluded more than fifty years earlier with the tribes of that area; but the Liberians had major difficulties with the Grebo tribesmen, who resided both in the disputed area and in Maryland County. Thus, they were incapable of resisting this French *fait accompli*. The final insult came over the deceptive wording of the treaty regarding the "right" and "left" banks of the Cavalla River. In the process the Liberians were tricked into accepting French control over the entire river. Furthermore, a boundary delimitation treaty in 1910 found the Liberians surrendering to the French their historic claims to a vast strip of land along the Guinea and Ivory Coast borders. In all, the British and French gained control of more than a third of the hinterland once claimed by the Americo-Liberians.

Not all the opposition to Americo-Liberian expansion was external. Elements within the settler community regarded expansion, especially by military means, with alarm. Not only did it curtail commerce and threaten the peace, but expansion might ultimately threaten the supremacy of the immigrant group in the new state. The intensity of internal opposition led to the resignation of at least one President, William D. Coleman in 1900, and forced several others to modify substantially their interior policies. Vestiges of this conservative approach have led many Americo-Liberians to oppose Tubman's Unification and Open-Door policies, on the grounds that they will open the floodgates and swamp the descendants of the settlers in a tribal sea.

Despite the whittling away of the Americo-Liberian claims in the interior, the settlers and their descendants eventually found themselves in possession of approximately 43,000 square miles of land.[13] Legal possession, however, was not the same as actual physical control. The Americo-Liberians, with only limited resources and technology at their command, found it difficult to build an effective system of roads into the interior. Indeed, the deep ravines that run at right angles to the coast, the tropical environment, and the extensive coastal mangrove swamps have made contact even among the Americo-Liberian coastal settlements a tenuous proposition. Forging inland beyond the forty-mile coastal plain required that one first penetrate a fairly dense tropical rain forest before reaching the interior plateau, a rolling expanse that averages approximately 800 to 1,000 feet in altitude, broken occasionally by small ranges of hills and outcroppings. The largest of the latter is Nimba Mountain (found in 1955 to be a major source of high-grade iron ore), which rises over 4,000 feet above sea level. The bulk of the Americo-Liberian population, then, remained clustered at the coast. Even today, despite the immense road and railroad construction of the Tubman period, there are still vast tribal areas in the interior where the writ of the Liberian government is very weak indeed. Nevertheless, migration from the tribal reserves has exposed the inhabitants to some of the economic and political developments of the modern Liberian state.

[13] Liberia is slightly larger than the American state of Indiana and is half the size of Ghana or Guinea and one-twentieth the size of the Congo (Kinshasa). Only nine African states, including neighboring Sierra Leone, are smaller.

The Seeds of Discord

Hostility between the Americo-Liberian community and the tribal people has been a feature of Liberian society almost from the first settlers' arrival. At the heart of conflict has been the issue of land. The initial misunderstanding was over the traditional African concept of land tenure, which is based upon use rather than ownership through purchase. This was compounded by the subsequent failure of the settlers or the American Colonization Society to pay even the low prices agreed upon; by the seizure of land for alleged insults against the colonists or for nonpayment of debts; and by constant disputes over land boundaries. The land question was subsequently complicated by the policies and practices in the use of native labor on the farms of Liberian settlers. The outrageous wage differentials, the lack of amenities, the unregulated power of farmers to "fine" their employees, and the abuses of the apprenticeship system under which young natives were assigned to Americo-Liberian families until they came of age created a situation in Africa not unlike the very one against which the repatriated Americo-Liberians had rebelled in America. The indigenous African, moreover, was expected to give freely of his labor for road construction and other public projects as well as to pay taxes to an alien government. Neither initial Liberian legislation nor the Constitution of 1847 recognized the taxed native as a citizen. Only the threat of European incursions into the hinterland compelled President Arthur Barclay in 1904 to extend citizenship to the tribal residents of the interior as proof of the effectiveness of Liberia's claim to the districts adjacent to Sierra Leone.

Many tribal groups (the Mandingoes in particular) resented the Americo-Liberian disruption of the slave trade and their ultimate monopoly over the commerce in cloth, molasses, and other more legitimate items. Finally, the settlers' arrogance in their relations with the indigenous inhabitants created a climate of hostility. The colonial rulings against nudity, the reluctance of the settler males to marry tribal women with whom they had established liaisons, the efforts at conversion to Christianity, and the patterns of segregation that emerged in housing and education demonstrated the settler's contempt for the tribal person and his culture.

Although over the years a certain amount of assimilation did take place among the two groups, the prescribed form of integration was decidedly on Americo-Liberian terms and conditional upon the acceptance by the tribal person of various facets of the settler culture, and not the reverse. Thus, English rather than pidgin or one of the sixteen tribal languages is the only legitimate medium of communication in official circles, in mission schools, and elsewhere. Christianity—preferably a Protestant version of it —displaced Islam or traditional forms of worship as the prescribed route to salvation. In the social realm, monogamy (or the "sequential monogamy" described previously) succeeded polygamy in the organization of the family. To play a role, the tribal person had to accept political and legal institutions that bear at least a formal resemblance to those of the United States. Moreover the tribesman had to accept—at least outwardly—the Americo-Liberian historical myth regarding the dominant role that the alien settlers and the negligible part that tribal people had played in the founding of the Republic. To the extent that he was permitted to participate in the economic sphere, the tribal person seeking assimilation had to embrace the concept of private rather than communal ownership of property, engage in a cash economy, and assume a large measure of individual rather than collective responsibility for his own prosperity. In general, the tribal person also had to accept the foods, dress, art, and architecture of the Americo-Liberians as the legitimate ideal.

Reinforcement of the Americo-Liberian Class

The tribal person who aspired to full participation in the new society found himself a largely unwelcome guest. The founding settlers of Liberia sought to swell their ranks not by converting the "heathen savages"—as the indigenous Africans were frequently called—but by encouraging other alien Negroes to emigrate to their shores. The Congoes, for example, found themselves preferred to the indigenous Africans, and they gradually acquired the manners and aspirations of the dominant settler group. By 1870 their passive role in Liberian politics was abandoned, and for a considerable time they occupied a pivotal position in the factional arguments developing within the Americo-Liberian group. Their ultimate affiliation with the ruling True Whig Party brought them to a position of near parity with the descendants of the American settlers, and today it is difficult to differentiate a Congo from other Americo-Liberians.

Recruitment from the New World, however, fell dramatically after the abolition of slavery and the passage of the Fourteenth and Fifteenth Amendments. Even the subsequent disillusionment with the degree and pace of the struggle for equality could not rekindle American Negro hopes for Liberia as an answer to their problems. Thus, they largely rejected Marcus Garvey and other more recent advocates of a "back to Africa" movement.[14] Those who did make it to Liberia from the New World following the American Civil War were from the West Indies. There was, for example, the band of three hundred and forty-six Barbadians who arrived in 1865. This group included the young Arthur Barclay, who ultimately founded one of the most remarkable family dynasties in Liberian history.[15] The West Indies also contributed Edward Wilmot Blyden, the scholar-statesman who contributed to the nineteenth-century history of both Liberia and Sierra Leone. Generally, however, the immigration from Haiti, Jamaica, and other parts of the West Indies has been steady but not numerically significant.

Further accretions to the ruling class have resulted from a small amount of African emigration from Ghana, Nigeria, Sierra Leone, and other African states. The King family of Sierra Leone, for example, eventually provided Liberia with a President and other distinguished public officials. The majority of immigrant Africans, however, associate more closely with the tribal Liberians than the Americo-Liberians, and they do not normally apply for naturalization. Indeed, African immigration is to a considerable extent offset by the emigration of Liberians to other parts of the continent. Clusters of Liberians, both tribal

[14] For the discussion of some very recent American Negro migration to Liberia, see Chapter 7.

[15] Arthur Barclay was President from 1904 to 1912. His descendants included President Edwin Barclay, various Justices of the Supreme Court, Senators, and Cabinet members as well as Mrs. W. V. S. Tubman.

and Americo-Liberian, can be found in Freetown, Lagos, and other cities along the West Coast.

The curious feature in the efforts of the Americo-Liberian class to strengthen its position within the Republic by adding to its numbers is that it so long rejected the notion of large-scale assimilation of the tribal people into its ranks. It has only been within the present century, indeed, within the presidency of William V. S. Tubman, that the tribal person has had a realistic chance of participating in the governing of his own country.

CHAPTER 2

Tribalism and
Traditionalism

The expansion of the Americo-Liberian community beyond the pockets of settlement at the coast created a highly
complex political, social, and economic situation. It was
not a simple case of one society dominating another.
Rather, it was a relationship that ultimately subordinated
sixteen or more tribal societies to the Western-oriented
community of Americo-Liberians. The dominated groups
differed radically in culture, degree of political cohesion
and organization, ability and resolution to resist Americo-
Liberian domination, and responsiveness to modernization. Lacking both the personnel and the anthropological
skills needed to carry out flexible and imaginative administrative policies in the tribal areas, the Americo-Liberian
leadership has been continually confounded by the character and variety of traditional tribal institutions. In the
present period of rapid change, understanding of the nature of tribal values and institutions by governmental
leadership is a *sine qua non* for survival.

Although the relative size of Liberia's tribal groupings
has undoubtedly undergone constant change since the days
of initial contact with the settler community, an indication
of the present-day numerical strength of the sixteen officially recognized tribes will be useful.[1] Only a few of the

[1] Linguists, missionaries, and others classify tribal groups in diverse

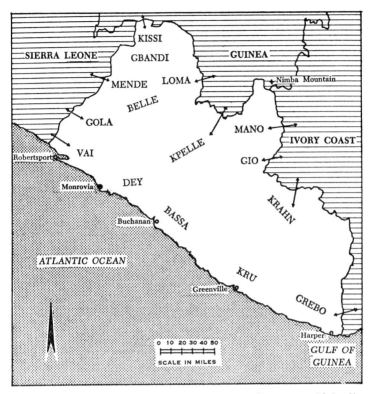

Distribution of Liberian tribal groups (Mandingo are widely distributed throughout the country)

groups, such as the Bassa, Belle, and Dey, are found almost entirely within Liberia. The majority of the sixteen straddle the borders between Liberia and the neighboring fashions. One count places the number of tribes at twenty-eight. The sixteen enumerated in the Census of Population of 1962 are indicated in Table 2, Chapter 2 of this volume. The "alien African tribes" in the table include 5,166 Fanti, most of whom are coastal fishermen and consider themselves citizens of Ghana.

states of Sierra Leone, Guinea, and the Ivory Coast. In some cases, such as the Mende, the major portion of the tribe resides across the border.

Table 2. Tribal affiliation of Liberia's population, 1962

Tribe	Size	Per cent
Kpelle	211,081	20
Bassa	165,856	16
Gio	83,208	8
Kru	80,813	8
Grebo	77,007	8
Mano	72,122	7
Loma	53,891	5
Krahn	52,552	5
Gola	47,295	5
Kissi	34,914	4
Mandingo	29,750	3
Vai	28,898	3
Gbandi	28,599	3
Belle	5,465	.5
Dey	5,396	.5
Mende	4,974	.5
Miscellaneous	2,299	.5
Total tribal	984,120	97
Alien African	8,875	1
No tribal affiliation	23,478	2
Total population	1,016,473	100

The integrity of tribal membership has been only slowly eroded over the century and a half of contact between the settlers and the indigenous inhabitants. Even today the majority of Liberia's residents identify much more strongly with their tribal communities than they do with the modern state of Liberia. There are, however, considerable ranges in the degree of response to Americo-Liberian cultural traits. The Dey and Bassa, who were settled behind Monrovia and Buchanan, early became involved in the settler economy as artisans, clerks, and domestic servants. The Vai, on the other hand, who also had early contact with the settlers in Cape Mount, proudly resisted submission to the taxing authority of the Liberian government until 1917. Individual Vai leadership, nevertheless, formed an aristocratic coalition with the Americo-Liberian leaders. By the beginning of the present century members of the Massaquoi, Fahnbulleh, and other Vai families (who skillfully moved from "pagan" to Muslim to Christian affiliations as the occasion demanded) were serving in the administration, the army officer cadre, and even the consular service. Similarly, despite sporadic resistance offered by various sections of the Grebo, mission-educated Grebo appeared as teachers, ministers, and even authors early in the 1900's.

An ambivalent case was that of the Kru, who continued their resistance into the 1930's, yet were the most cash-minded group along the coast. Indeed, more than a century before the Americo-Liberian arrival the Krus were trading with passing European vessels. For many decades now the Kru have regularly served as crewmen and stevedores for European and American freighters plying the West Coast of Africa. The Gola and Mandingo, too, have had an ambivalent relationship with the Americo-Liberians. Their long history of contact was constantly disturbed by the commercial rivalry between the settlers and these two groups who had dominated the trade in slaves and legitimate items in northwestern Liberia. The unusual strength of the Poro secret society among the Gola (discussed later in this chapter) and the Islamic faith of the Mandingoes, moreover, served as barriers to rapid assimilation of these two tribal groups.

In the remote hinterland of Liberia contact has been limited largely to the present century. Indeed, the Mano, Gio, Loma, and Krahn have really only had their traditional patterns of life substantially threatened during the years since the Second World War as missionaries, new economic enterprises, and the network of roads and railroads have penetrated inland. Already the rich artistic tradition of the Gio and Mano in the fields of wood sculpture, weaving, dancing, and music is giving way to the enameled pots, readymade shirts, and "high life" musical records brought north by the Lebanese traders. The Loma and Krahn, too, have been exposed to the Americo-Liberian political system through their involvement in the army. Perhaps the least acculturated group in the country is the largest—the Kpelle. Even among these people, however, the pace of life is rapidly changing as the recruiters for the rubber plantations seek new labor markets and as the iron-mining concessions locate within their midst.

The Arrival and Dispersal of Liberian Tribes

Given the underdeveloped state of archaeological studies in the West Atlantic region of Africa, it is difficult to assert with any confidence when the earliest human settlement took place in Liberia. Oral tradition in most tribal groups confirms that the present inhabitants are descendants of fairly recent arrivals in Liberia. It is possible that four or five centuries ago the area of what is today Sierra Leone and Liberia was largely uninhabited tropical rain forest. The great upheavals of the fifteenth and sixteenth centuries associated with the rise, flourishing, and eventual collapse of the Songhai Empire on the Niger River changed matters. A series of crises drove waves of non-Moslems into the forest region. The advent of the European merchants at the coast further disturbed the political and economic balances in West Africa. The patterns of trade—especially with respect to human cargo—were dramatically reoriented. Thus, over a three-hundred-year span there was a movement of Mande-speaking people into Liberia from the north, various West Atlantic-speaking people from the Futa Jalon to the northwest, and Kwa-speaking peoples from the east and southeast. The Dutch trader Olfert Dapper reported in 1686 that the Dey tribe had already reached the Atlantic and controlled the area between the mouth of the Mesurado River and the Mano River. The Dey were in vague alliance with the Vai, who occupied the coastal strip to the west. The Gola tribesmen were expanding into the inland area behind the Vai.[2]

The major Liberian tribal groups reached their present locations about the time that the Americo-Liberian settlers landed near Monrovia. The period immediately preceding

[2] In presenting the material in this chapter, I am indebted to the assistance provided by Mr. Robert Luneburg, currently a graduate student in political science at Indiana University, who spent two years in Liberia. I have drawn heavily upon the Ph.D. dissertations of James Gibbs on the Kpelle and Warren d'Azevedo on the Gola as well as other writings of these scholars. The citations appear in the Bibliographic Essay at the end of this volume. I have also used extensively the published works of the late George Harley, George Schwab, Svend Holsoe, and other ethnographers as well as several monographs produced by the Liberian Bureau of Folkways. The authors of the government monographs are not identified in the publications.

the nineteenth century was apparently marked by a constant series of movements, with stronger tribal groupings driving weaker ones farther into the rain forest or down the coast. Indeed, there has always been a certain amount of fluctuation of tribal boundaries. The constant search for new agricultural lands or the flight from tax collectors, labor recruiters, and arbitrary rulers have constantly driven people into previously uninhabited and uncharted sections of Liberia. Artificial and largely unregulated international boundaries have provided no obstacle to Mende, Gola, Kissi, and Vai, who move back and forth to renew old ties with kinsmen in Sierra Leone; to Grebo, Kru, and Krahn who visit their relatives in the Ivory Coast; or to Loma, Kpelle, Mandingo, Mano, and Gio who have maintained their economic and social links with kinsmen in Guinea.

Significance of Tribal Membership

It is difficult to assess the historical contribution each tribal group has made to the development of modern Liberia or the magnitude of the threat each posed to the Americo-Liberian settlers in the nineteenth century. Even the classification of Liberia's people into neat tribal compartments has been an extremely complicated task. Ethnic identity has not been coterminous with political affiliation. A major group such as the Kpelle, for example, has consisted of a great many relatively autonomous political units living on both sides of the Liberian and Guinean borders. On the other hand, some of the political confederacies of the nineteenth century temporarily brought together people of various ethnic origins. Classification of Liberia's population into three language groups is of little value for political analysis, and it certainly does not tell us very

Table 3. Linguistic classification of Liberian tribal groups

Mande–speaking peoples	West Atlantic–speaking peoples	Kwa–speaking peoples
Western Branch	*Southern Branch*	*Kru branch*
Mandingo (Malinke)	Gola	Bassa
Vai	Kissi (Gissi)	Dey (De)
Gbandi (Gbande)		Grebo (Glebo)
Kpelle (Kpessi)		Kru (Krou)
Loma (Buzi)		Belle
Mende		Krahn
Eastern Branch		
Gio (Dan)		
Mano (Ma)		

Based on U.S. Army, *Area Handbook for Liberia* (U.S. Govt. Printing Office, Dept. of Army, Pamphlet No. 550–38, p. 51. Adapted from Joseph Greenberg and the Diedrich Westermann and Margaret A. Bryan articles cited in the Bibliographic Essay.

much about the way people actually identified with one another for social, economic, and political purposes.[3] Finally, there is the problem of nomenclature, with a number of fairly distinct tribal people having the same group name, whereas a single grouping may refer to them-

[3] Joseph Greenberg's classification in 1963 designated all of the languages of the area as Niger–Congo. They were subdivided into three genetic subfamilies: West Atlantic (Gola, Kisi), Kwa–speaking Kru Branch (Bassa, Dey, Grebo, Kru, Belle, Krahn), and Eastern and Western branches of the Mande–speaking peoples (Western: Mandingo, Vai, Gbandi, Kpelle, Loma, and Mende; Eastern: Gio, Mano). See Greenberg, "The Languages of Africa," *International Journal of American Linguistics,* XXIX, no.1 part two (1963), 8. Other works on Liberian languages are cited in the Bibliographic Essay at the end of this volume.

selves by one name but be given other titles by their various neighbors.

Perhaps the best that we can say is that tribal membership in Liberia is a conscious state of "belonging," which permits a group of people to identify with each other and differentiate themselves from third parties on the basis of a broad configuration of common factors. Among the factors would be language; the common occupation of some historical "homeland"; recognition of a set of mutual interests that are worth defending against both external and internal threats; solidarity and cooperation in a range of economic and social transactions; similar customs and ways of looking at the world; and even political unity. A given tribal grouping may lack any one of these factors, but the broad character of the configuration permits the individual to give priority to the many overlapping and even conflicting membership groupings of which he may be a part.

Parochial Character of Tribal Society

The most striking feature of tribal society in Liberia has been the highly parochial character of social, economic, and political activity. Aside from the Mandingo-dominated kingdom of Kondo at Bopolu, Liberia had nothing resembling the complex trading kingdoms found elsewhere in West Africa. There were no urban clusters of any consequence in the region until the arrival of the Americo-Liberians. Apparently the problems of defense, limited technology, the extraordinary land requirements of shifting cultivation (which permits worn-out fields to lie fallow and revert to bush for several years), and the difficulties of taming the tropical rain forest militated against the concentration of people in urban settings.

The process of political and social decentralization of authority was most severe among the coastal Kru and among the Grebo and Krahn in the southeast. The most that could be found there were clusters of villages or towns, few of which numbered over several hundred inhabitants. Within these small units, most of the political, social, and economic transactions of traditional tribal society took place. The Gola, Mende, Vai, Loma, and Kpelle in the north and west were organized into larger units under chiefs. As noted above, however, the tribe was broken into a number of relatively autonomous units. The Vai, for example, are divided into nine chiefdoms, only four of which are located in Liberia. The political fragmentation among the larger Kpelle community is far greater.

Involvement in more cosmopolitan associations within a single tribe or even cutting across tribal lines took place on a sporadic rather than a sustained basis. That is, warfare brought people into contact with their neighbors for the purposes of resisting or committing aggression. Trading with the itinerant Mandingoes gave a parochial community occasional vicarious economic contact with peoples on the other side of the Sahara. George Brown, the American economist, reported in 1941 that an elaborate system of markets, involving the exchange of woven cloth and other commodities, had developed among the Loma and adjacent northwestern tribes. Although contemporary scholars have questioned the complexity of these markets, there was undoubtedly an exchange economy in which the twisted iron bars (called Kissi pennies) served as currency. Another cross-community tie was the journeys that tribesmen took to their parent villages in order to strengthen family and other bonds which had been permitted to lapse. Finally, the religious and mystical ties provided by the

Poro, Sande, and other secret societies brought communities together for limited purposes.

The basic building block of tribal society has been the nuclear family, consisting of a man, his wife or wives, and his offspring. Also considered part of certain households in the past were the pawns, slaves, apprentices, and other people who had voluntarily or otherwise found themselves in the protective custody of important men in a community. The practice of pawning was widespread throughout West Africa. Under this system a man placed one of his relatives (and occasionally himself) in servitude until a debt had been paid. The greater the size of a man's retinue, the greater his prestige in the community.

Unlike many groupings in East Africa and occasional groups in West Africa where matrilineal rules of family membership and inheritance prevail, the tribes of Liberia have subscribed to a patrilineal system of reckoning family obligation. The family has been the most significant social unit for a Liberian tribesman, for birth into a particular patrilineal kinship group gives one legitimacy, support in time of crisis, and companionship. Throughout his lifetime, however, an individual might be involved with more than one such kinship unit. Polygamy plus the rules of exogamy, which demand marriage outside one's own kinship group, establish an expanding number of marital ties with women of other kin groups. Thus, in the traditional period the overlapping ties of kinship created by marriage provided a mechanism for resolving conflicts even in those political units without formal structures of government.

The family household has also been the most important economic unit in tribal society. The growing and processing of rice, cassava, and other staple crops has been a family enterprise, with the food produced being largely consumed by the family. Similarly, the products gathered in the forest, the meat and hides secured in the hunt, or the fish caught in the rivers or the sea have been processed by the family. There have been, however, certain exceptions to the parochial character of traditional economic activity. The bartering of the few surplus agricultural commodities and the sale of slaves did permit cultivators to acquire the hoes, cloth, and other commodities made by craft specialists or brought into the community by Mandingo traders. Among the Mano, Kpelle, and other tribes, labor cooperatives, or kuus, supplemented the basic family work group in larger villages. A kuu consisted of households who combined: [4]

for the purpose of working in rotation on the farms of members, because they believed that they worked harder and with more enjoyment when in a group. Kuus could be of men, women, or mixed. A household would contribute as many members as it was able. The number of days a kuu would work for each member was determined by a vote at the organizational meeting. Usually the kuu worked two full days for every member. Thus a household would receive two kuu days for every worker it contributed. Kuus were formed newly each season and were involved in such work as clearing forest, scratching and planting and harvesting. Only work which had a constant output could be organized into kuus. This ruled out all forms of production where an element of chance was involved, such as hunting or fishing.

[4] David Blanchard, "The Development of Small Farm Agriculture in Liberia," U.S.AID, Monrovia, 31 July 1967, pp. 6–7 (mimeographed).

Just as the economic and social patterns have been both
local and kinship-based, so have the patterns of political
affiliation focused upon the family and the parochial community. Indeed, in certain instances in the past the family
unit served double duty as the social and political unit.
Migration or other action that severed the day-to-day ties
of individuals with their parent villages permitted or
compelled the heads of families to constitute their own
political communities. Although initially ties might be
maintained on an intermittent basis as migrants returned
"home" to attend funerals, have their children initiated
into the tribe, or claim an inheritance, eventually the
hived-off community attained a political significance of its
own, and the head of the family served also as the political
chief.

It is not suggested that the family political community
was either typical or normal outside the tribes of the
southeast (the Kru, Grebo, and Krahn). The family-based
chiefdom among the Kpelle or Gola did not usually remain small for very long. It would expand as the sons of
the founders took wives from other villages or as migrating
strangers were granted permission to farm upon their acceptance of the political authority of the founding head-
man or his heir, often referred to as the "owner of the
land." Gradually a cluster of kin-related villages might be
grouped with similar clusters to form "towns." When this
occurred the original clusters would be regarded as wards,
or quarters, each under the authority of a senior kinsman.
The quarter chief would have special responsibilities for
the safety and good order of the quarter; he inaugurated
the agricultural cycle and was custodian of properties belonging to the corporate kinship group. One of the pri-

mary duties of a quarter chief was the reassignment of land
that had earlier been parcelled out on a usufructuary right-
of-occupancy basis. The quarter chief also organized community work projects and settled disputes involving not
only his own kinsmen but also members of "stranger" kinship groups. The quarter chief had to be cautious in dealing with the interests of all groups in the community, and
he was required to work through a council of elders, each
of whom jealously guarded the rights and prerogatives of
his particular family segment. Any elder who repeatedly
became dissatisfied with the actions of a quarter chief
could physically withdraw his family from the jurisdiction
of the autocrat and establish a new political community.

At the town level, predominantly political institutions
emerged, for impartial authorities were required to settle
disputes among contesting kinship groupings. Succession
to a town chieftainship was largely hereditary, but it often
rotated among a series of leading families with equal
claims of seniority, prestige, or wealth. Although town
chiefs could act arbitrarily with respect to quarter chiefs
and other subordinate officials, the council of elders attained a more structured bureaucratic character at the
town level than it had achieved at the quarter level. In certain tribal areas the young men's age-grade societies also
became more significant at this level of the political system, and a town chief had to contend with a corporate
grouping that cut across kinship lines and shared his executive, legislative, and judicial functions. The young
men's "house of representatives" played a vital role in
some (but certainly not all) tribal societies in defense as
well as in the control of the social behavior of its members.
The primary sanction for the authority of the town chief

probably stemmed from the belief that he was more impartial in his justice than the locally rooted quarter chief
and yet not as remote from affairs as the chief of the next
higher level, the clan.

"Clan" Chieftainship

The term *clan* in Liberian usage is deceptive, since it re-
fers to a territorial unit rather than to a kinship grouping.
The clan was typically the largest political entity among
the various tribes of Liberia, even though larger, more
ephemeral political groupings did exist. The Americo-
Liberians, moreover, undermined the supremacy of clan
chieftainship by grouping various clan units into so-called
paramount chieftaincies. In the traditional period the clan
consisted of a number of towns, villages, and hamlets
joined together for political purposes as a result of migrants having settled in the same area, as a consequence of
defensive alliances becoming permanent, or through normal expansion of towns where the common bonds of kinship and tribe were strong. In some cases, a noted warrior
chief would be invited to assume the leadership of weaker
chiefdoms incapable of defending themselves. The suzerainty of the warrior chief was invariably sealed by his marriage to the daughters of the leading town chiefs and other
"big men" of his area. Gola warrior clan chiefs, for example, often left the existing town and quarter structures intact, demanding only tribute in the form of rice, women,
labor, and soldiers. In many instances, however, the warrior chief set up his own bureaucracy with a retinue of his
relatives and mercenaries imported to administer the consolidated area.

The clan chief, or petty paramount chief, was the secular ruler of his area. He organized the defense of the clan, called the people out for work on major public projects such as forts, bridges, and paths, and supervised the executive actions of the town chiefs. The clan chief heard cases on appeal, where an offended party did not feel that justice had been rendered by a town chief. For his efforts the chief was remunerated by tribute payments, court fees, and a share of the meat secured in a tribal hunt. He used his wealth to increase his stature in the community. This was done directly by sharing his rice, cloth, and even junior wives with a series of clients, who served as his claque and sang his praises. Indirectly, by giving the appearance of generosity and meeting the needs of the community in times of crisis, a clan chief could establish a reputation that would attract new settlers into his chieftaincy. Thus, the base from which he could secure additional wealth as well as soldiers expanded in proportion to his patronage, and the chief's generosity was an important factor in community solidarity in traditional tribal society.

Succession to the office of clan chief seldom rigidly followed hereditary rules of succession, even though preference was normally given to the sons, brothers, and paternal cousins of the late chief. On occasion a son of the late chief's sister or even the sister herself could succeed to office. Experience did play a significant role in the actual selection by the elders, who sought someone who had displayed military skills, had demonstrated eloquence and impartiality in the settlement of a dispute, or could lead without resorting to force. Wealth also played a role, and a "big man" with a large clientage might get himself elected to the clan chieftainship. This was not really regarded as objectionable since a chief was expected to display generosity, and the chief who lived poorly might be jealous of those who were more prosperous than himself.

The size of clan chiefdoms varied considerably and fluctuated as a result of normal increase and conquest. The size of a chiefdom might diminish as discontented elements hived off into the forest in search of new lands and freedom, as mercenaries switched their allegiances from a stingy and unsuccessful chief, or as traders and other specialists severed their client relationships with clan chiefs who became too demanding or could not furnish adequate protection for commerce. It was largely in western Liberia that the scale of the political community reached considerable proportions. There, a number of confederacies involving people from more than one ethnic group were brought into existence for purposes of warfare and trade. As enduring political units, however, they were relatively unstable.

Religion and Social Control

Not all of the restraints upon political leadership or upon mass deviant behavior were secular. There was a continual resort to supernatural mechanisms in controlling the operation of the political system. Magic, for example, has been a very persistent and effective means for securing social control or disruption. Furthermore, a chief might find his secular authority challenged by the religious authority of the "owner of the land." The latter was a descendant of the founder of the community and performed ritual functions in behalf of the whole chiefdom in time of crisis. The "owner of the land" also might be called upon to settle disputes between the secular chief and the officials of the secret societies.

Generally, those tribes, such as the Vai and Gola, whose traditional religious system included a high god, tended to regard the deity as benevolent and remote from the affairs of men. Man attempted to manipulate his fate, or had his fate manipulated, through the actions of either important ancestral spirits or nature spirits that inhabited the cotton-wood trees, rivers, or rocks. Through sacrifice and rituals performed by paid specialists, called *zoes,* a man attempted to secure the success of his harvest or a journey and perhaps bring disaster upon his political, commercial, or matrimonial rivals. The position of *zoe* was normally inherited, and there were both male and female specialists. Other individuals sought prominence through their membership in the Baboon, Leopard, and other societies that practiced ritualistic murder. Although membership in such societies was supposedly secret, a member gained influence if it was popularly assumed that he belonged to such an organization.

Two secret societies constituted the greatest supernatural mechanisms for controlling both deviant behavior on the part of the peasantry and autocratic tendencies on the part of political leaders. The men's Poro and women's Sande societies represent a distinct cultural feature of the West Atlantic region. The Poro is most highly developed among the Gola, and they are alleged to be the source of Poro authority among the Vai and Dey. Secret societies of varying strength are found among the Kpelle, Mano, Kissi, Gbandi, Gbunde, Belle, Loma, Gio, and the Mende. The Mende claim to have originated the Poro in the tribes farther west, in Sierra Leone. Indeed, the only people without the Poro in the past were the Bassa, Kru, and Mandingo. Among the Poro-oriented tribal groups, the rituals and sanctions of these secret societies took precedence over those of any other association or institution within the community. A chief often based his authority on his high rank within the Poro or the backing of the Poro officials. On important community matters, a chief would defer to the council of the Poro. The council consisted of old men who had attained the highest of the approximately one hundred degrees, or orders, of the Poro society. Meeting in the sacred grove, the council could reverse the decision of a chief and even depose and dispose of an errant chief who did not himself hold high status within the Poro.

In political terms the Poro has been among the most significant of integrative forces within Gola, Kpelle, Mano, and other tribal groups. Its sacred bonds cut across the vertical kinship divisions within a community and bridged the geographic gaps separating various segments of a tribal community. Although loose in structure and only operating from time to time, the Poro could link otherwise autonomous chiefdoms within a single ethnic grouping. This occurred among the fragmented Gola, for example, as they expanded at the expense of their neighbors in the precontact period. There is also evidence that the Poro could provide a measure of cohesion that cut across even tribal lines. Warren D'Azevedo, for example, commented that even today the Dey people await permission of Gola Poro officials before opening a new society. There has also been a great deal of intertribal exchange of ritual as young Poro members from one tribe have been apprenticed to powerful *zoes*, of another tribe. There is some disagreement, however, over the actual strength of the intertribal network of the Poro in Liberia. The late George Harley insisted that the highest officials of the various chapters of the Poro were bound together in some kind of supreme council. There is no historical evidence, however, that the trans-tribal links in Liberia reached the stage where the Poro could present a united intertribal front against the Americo-Liberian penetration of the hinterland. In Sierra Leone, on the other hand, the Mende-based Poro was able to unite several tribes in an abortive attempt to prevent British expansion into the interior of Sierra Leone in 1898.[5]

For most purposes the Liberian Poro appears to have been effective largely at the local level. The Poro societies, for example, were prominent during the traditional era in controlling such antisocial behavior as incest, murder, arson, and looting by warriors, as well as for ensuring positive cooperation in matters of defense, cultivation, house-building, bridge construction, and other community projects. In cooperation with the Sande, the Poro controlled the behavior of women generally and of women "chiefs" in particular while the young warriors were absent from the community. The primary sanction of the Poro was the fear and awe that the visit of one of the masked figures instilled in the women, children, and un-initiated youths. The ultimate sanction of the Poro was the death penalty, which could be meted out to those who committed serious offenses against society or revealed the secrets of the Poro. Since the mask rather than the unidentified wearer was responsible for the death sentence and execution, there could be no claims for compensation filed by the kinsmen of the victim; the mask, or the spirits pre-

[5] Kenneth Little, "The Political Function of the Poro," *Africa,* XXXV (Oct. 1965), 349–365; and Vernon Dorjahn, "The Initiation of Temne Poro Officials," *Man,* LXI (Feb. 1961), 36 ff.

sumed to reside in the mask, belonged to no kinship group, and its actions thus were ritually sanctioned. The rituals performed in relation to the pantheon of masks provided bonds of community solidarity far stronger than any secular bonds of mere economic or social cooperation.

The Poro and Sande societies, moreover, have continued to be among the most important socializing agencies in the tribal community, and the Liberian government tolerates their activities today if they do not interfere with Western-type schools, clinics, or other institutions. At extended intervals—frequently when a chief's young son reaches puberty—the young boys and girls are sent off to separate bush schools for four- and three-year periods, respectively. During their seclusion the children are instructed in tribal lore and the secrets of the Poro or Sande. They are also taught marital responsibilities, the uses of herbs and other medicines, techniques of agriculture, and other matters relating to their adult roles in society. At the end of the confinement and indoctrination the initiate becomes in effect a new member of the community. This is symbolized by the taking of a new name and by tribal markings on the body. Although the boys have, in many instances, undergone circumcision prior to the bush school, clitoridectomy is usually performed on the young girls by an official of the Sande society during the period of seclusion.

Granting the positive aspects of the integrative and socializing functions of the Poro, the resort to the supernatural in controlling behavior casts some doubt on the proposition that traditional tribal government was essentially democratic. George Harley argued, however, that the resort to masks and ordeals was a stand-by measure, which came into play only when the family structures, the council of elders, and other secular controls upon both autocracy and mass antisocial behavior failed. "In the last analysis," Harley said, "it was government by tradition, enforced by the fear of disapproval of the ancestors. Decisions were reached with the approval of the clan fathers both living and dead. The living merely used a technique, placing both the responsibility for these decisions and the blame for the administration of justice on the ancestral spirits." [6] Thus stability was maintained in a highly fragile and fragmented society.

Summary

To the Americo-Liberian district commissioner, the American missionary, and the Lebanese shopkeeper, an appreciation of the subtle distinctions in values and institutions among the sixteen or more tribal groups of Liberia spells the difference between success or failure in their efforts to change traditional societies in the Liberian hinterland. It is impossible in this brief summary to do full justice to the great cultural variations among and even within the Gola, Kpelle, and other Liberian tribes. Nevertheless, it is hoped that this synopsis has pointed out the ways in which tribal societies in general differ from (and resemble) the Americo-Liberian community that dominates their affairs. Perhaps the one outstanding feature has been the small scale of the effective community within each of the tribal groups and the crucial role played by the extended patrilineal family in organizing the political, social, and economic affairs within the fragmented tribal societies. Another feature that has plagued the Americo-

[6] "Masks as Agents of Social Control in Northeast Liberia," *Papers of the Peabody Museum,* XXXII, no. 2 (1950), x–xi.

Liberians as they extended inland has been the tribal attitude toward land tenure, which is based upon use and need rather than upon private ownership. Furthermore, the religious and ritualistic base for political authority— especially among the northwestern tribes where the Poro are or have been strong—has provided a basis for conflict between tribal authorities and the Protestant Americo-Liberians.

Finally, some comment is required on the tribal antipathy toward change. Traditional society has been essentially concerned with consensus rather than conflict, even though intercommunity warfare was a fairly common event. No society is static. Nevertheless, traditional society reacts to a major crisis by attempting through various mechanisms to restore equilibrium and to get things back to the way they were before the human or supernatural disaster disrupted the usual order of events. The extension of Americo-Liberian influence inland, however, constituted a permanent challenge to the equilibrium of traditional society in the Liberian hinterland.

CHAPTER 3

Punishment, Persuasion, and Party Politics

The supremacy of the settlers and their descendants over the tribal people has been maintained in a number of ways. Until the Tubman administration the primary device was coercive sanctions. With some tribal groups, such as the Grebo and Kru, this was understandable, for they accepted Americo-Liberian authority only after its military superiority had been demonstrated time and again in pitched battles. The superior numbers of the tribal people and the bitterness of the conflict forced the Liberian leaders to rely heavily upon physical force in securing compliance with their orders.

It was perhaps inevitable that the need to employ force in some areas led to its general use in areas where it was not required. The posting of a contingent of the militia or the Liberian Frontier Force to disturbed areas was all too frequently a measure of first, rather than last, resort in the maintenance of authority. If the area was not actually disturbed before the arrival of the troops, the prophecy of chaos was soon fulfilled. The remarks of President Arthur Barclay in his 1904 Inaugural Address that the militia—largely lower-class Americo-Liberians and tribal people drawn from areas other than those in which they were serving—was "tending to become a greater danger to the loyal citizen, and his property, which it ought to protect, than to the public enemy" have recent echoes in the pages of *Liberian Age* and the annual reports of district commissioners. The commissioner in Sanniquellie in 1960, for example, complained that the enlisted men, because of "lack of leadership, live an inebriated life, undisciplined, and mostly dishonest." [1] It has apparently long been the custom of the Frontier Force to live off the local community as much as traffic will bear.

In addition to direct physical force, obligations vis-à-vis the state have been imposed upon the tribal element that constitute at least a formal recognition of the superiority of the Liberian government. The hut tax, although only sporadically enforced in the early period, has become a recurrent obligation. The tribal people also are compelled by law to render service to the central government and to the chiefs in the construction of roads and in carrying out other community projects. Furthermore, forcible recruitment into the Liberian Frontier Force is an ever-present threat to restive individuals within a tribal community.

Besides the legal coercive sanctions, extralegal exactions imposed upon the tribal people by both officials and civilians drove home the lesson of Americo-Liberian supremacy. President Tubman's executive councils in the hinterland have brought to light practices that in the previous administrations went unpunished and often unnoticed. The tribal people had previously felt powerless to complain when special unauthorized taxes were levied by the district commissioners or when they were forced to work for little or no pay upon the farms of officials and prominent private Americo-Liberians. They had no re-

[1] Liberia, Department of the Interior, *Annual Report,* 1959–1960, pp. 26–27.

course, moreover, when officials acquired tribal consorts or wives without the payment of dowry. Only during the Tubman administration has an attempt been made to regularize and limit the use of compulsory labor.

Another category of negative sanctions calculated to maintain Americo-Liberian supremacy has been the control over residence and population movements. An extreme example has been the deportation from their home areas of politically restive tribe members and their confinement in one of the more remote districts of the interior.[2] Of a more general character has been the attempt to restrict intertribal contact by establishing tribal land units under traditional authority, similar to the reserve policy followed by the British in East Africa and still utilized by the whites in South Africa. A member of the group has a right to land in his tribal area, but a tribal stranger may take up residence only with the permission of the traditional leadership and upon the stranger's acceptance of the local chief's political authority. Also by way of population control, the Liberian government will not tolerate the mass exodus of a community from its traditional tribal area to avoid obligations or to diminish the strength of an unpopular chief. The government has taken steps to discourage the flight from their families and farms by males wishing to take advantage of the gold and diamond discoveries of the postwar period. The drift of tribal people to Monrovia and other urban centers has been countered by the city courts, which have taken drastic steps to return tribal vagrants to the hinterland. Furthermore, the

[2] A recent example of this occurred in Tchien District (Department of the Interior, *Annual Report,* 1955–1956, p. 15, and *Annual Report,* 1956–1957, p. 16).

Kru, Bassa, and other tribal migrants employed in Monrovia have been organized into separate residential communities for administrative and judicial purposes.

In addition to restrictions upon the movement of tribal people, the government attempted in the past to minimize contact between the indigenous population and outside influences. True, it was recognized that the European and Liberian missionaries or the Lebanese traders could teach certain aspects of the culture the Americo-Liberians had established as the norm for the whole state. Moreover, the establishment of Christian mission stations at Bolahun, Ganta, and other points far in the interior had served as bulwarks against the southward penetration of Mandingo and other Muslims into Liberia. Nevertheless, the teachings and actions of the European stranger could undermine the authority of the Liberian government. This was no idle fear. Disputes between missionaries over proselytizing areas, attacks by the Swedish Evangelical Lutherans upon the Poro and secret societies described in the preceding chapter, and the antagonism aroused by European commercial interests have posed real problems for the Liberian government in the maintenance of peace and order in the interior during the past and present centuries. Although aliens are no longer required to have an authorized pass to enter the provinces, there are still both legal and tacit restrictions upon the residence and activities of aliens in the hinterland.[3]

Indirect Rule in the Hinterland

The settlers and their descendants also hoped to maintain control over the tribal majority through the develop-

[3] See *Liberian Code of Laws of 1956* (Ithaca, N.Y.: Cornell University Press, 1957), title 15, ch. 12C, secs. 301–303.

ment of an efficient administrative service. To that end the Department of the Interior (now the Department of Internal Affairs) was created in 1868 during the presidency of James Spriggs Payne. For many decades, however, the effectiveness of the Department was blunted by the lack of qualified Americo-Liberians interested in living in the hinterland and by the difficulties that geography posed for the systematic supervision of the administrative officers. Moreover, there was clearly no explicit policy regarding both the ultimate goals of the dependency relationship and the means whereby the relationship was to be maintained or transformed. It was only during the administration of Arthur Barclay in the first decade of the present century that the Liberian government acknowledged that the tribal people of the hinterland were citizens of the Republic. Not until then were steps taken to establish a more efficient administrative service. Unfortunately, the stimulus for these policy decisions was the charge of the British and French that historic Liberian claims to territory could not be recognized in the absence of "effective occupation." Had the impetus for change come from within the Americo-Liberian community, the reforms might have been more meaningful.

The administrative system introduced by Barclay was patterned along the lines of "indirect rule": the utilization of traditional tribal authorities as instruments of the central government in the maintenance of law and order at the local level. Aside from the savings in money and personnel, this policy had many advantages for the Americo-Liberian minority. In the first place, it perpetuated the social division of the hinterland into more than twenty tribal groups and capitalized upon the existing political fragmentation of the majority of these tribal groups into relatively autonomous chiefdoms. Even though the creation of consolidated paramount chieftainships reversed the process of fragmentation to a certain degree, only the Dey, Mende, Gbandi, Kissi, and Belle people have been united under single paramount chiefs. In the other groups, political authority within a tribe is divided among as many as five paramount chiefs. Moreover, in drawing district boundaries, little respect was accorded tribal lines. Thus, the Kpelle have been dispersed among four administrative areas, whereas fragments of several mutually hostile tribes have been incorporated within single districts.

Despite the lack of respect for the integrity of a tribe as a social or political unit, local government has been essentially tribal in character. Where possible, tribal customs and institutions were preserved and utilized by the district commissioner in carrying out central government objectives. Thus, in many areas a modified form of hereditary succession to chieftainship has prevailed to the present day. Chiefs and elders at all levels administer customary law in the settlement of disputes concerning a wide range of social and economic relationships. Tribal membership has been further strengthened by the legalizing of the Poro and other secret societies, which in the early period were banned as potential political threats to Americo-Liberian rule. Corporate membership in the clan or other tribal unit is emphasized not only by the system of land tenure but also by the Liberian government's practice of levying fines against a whole community in the settlement of boundary disputes or failure to provide laborers for public projects. The political stability that resulted from the policy of recognizing native traditions even prompted the Americo-Liberians until 1930 to countenance the institutions of domestic slavery and the pawning of persons in the tribal areas.

The Liberian commitment to indirect rule has been of a pragmatic rather than a philosophic nature. No attempt was made, as Sir Donald Cameron had done in Tanganyika, to justify indirect rule as the morally best colonial system, the least damaging to the native personality in the transition from traditional to modern society. Native institutions in the Liberian hinterland have flourished only to the extent that they did not conflict with the interests of the Americo-Liberians. A chief, for example, might be chosen in a time-honored fashion; nevertheless, he was elected and held office only at the pleasure of the President. Similarly, the Poro has survived only on sufferance. The expediency of the Liberian policy is revealed as well in the attitude toward bush schools, in which tribal youth have been instructed in tribal lore and custom. Now that the central government has taken a more active interest in the educational programs of the interior, restrictions are being placed upon the traditional system of tribal indoctrination. The fate of the *zoes* and other practitioners of native medicine likewise will be conditional upon the rate at which programs in modern medicine expand in the hinterland.

The Single Party and the Role of Dissent

In defending their claims to govern the tribal people of the hinterland, the Americo-Liberian leaders had to concern themselves not merely with the twin threats posed by resistance of the tribal people and by the competing claims of the British and French in the neighboring colonies. Of equal danger to minority rule was the possibility of dissension within the ranks of the Americo-Liberian community weakening it during a moment of crisis. Thus, means had to be found to control the intense interest in politics and the tendency toward factionalism that has characterized Americo-Liberian society. The ultimate solution to this problem was the emergence of a single dominant party, which has maintained the solidarity of the settler community in the face of both internal and external threats for almost a century. Although dramatically different in its purpose and ideology from other contemporary dominant parties in Africa, the True Whig Party of Liberia inadvertently became the prototype for what is now a fairly typical institution in postindependence Africa.

An all-absorbing interest in politics and the organization of protest along factional lines have been evident in settler society almost from the establishment of the colony in 1822. The Remonstrance of December 5, 1823, regarding the allocation of house plots in the settlement at Mesurado, provided the American Colonization Society with concrete evidence that the settlers were not entirely content with paternalistic government. The Remonstrance compelled the Society to publish the Plan of Civil Government of 1824, which set forth the powers of the Board of Agents with respect to the colonists. During most of the first decade, however, the acceptable political activity of the Americo-Liberians was limited to the right of assembly and petition and to the election of a vice-agent and two councilors, who were to advise the agent in the administration of the colony. The election of settlers to fill these three posts turned largely on the personal qualifications of the candidates.

In the election of 1830, a decided split in the settler community arose between those supporting and those op-

posing the Colonization Society's administration of the settlements. This tendency of elections to revolve more and
more around issues rather than personalities became even
more apparent as the number of elective offices increased.
By 1835 a cleavage of interest became manifest between
the more conservative agricultural groups in the upper settlements and the more liberal and commercial elements in
and around Monrovia. It was not until the Commonwealth period (1839–1847), during which the settlers
achieved a measure of self-government prior to independence, that a rudimentary party system actually emerged.
The Reverend John Seys, who had been personally
offended by Governor Buchanan's policy on the entry of
duty-free goods for missionaries, organized an opposition
party that conducted its attack on a number of fronts: in
the legislative chamber, in public meetings, and through
the columns of Seys' newspaper, *Africa's Luminary*. Seys
criticized the administration for its policies and actions in
the fields of health, relations with the native chiefs, foreign
commerce, and taxation. Despite Seys' fanatic following
and its occasional resorts to violence, the Seys faction
found itself unable to dislodge the Monrovia group from
control of the Commonwealth Legislature. Buchanan's
successor, Joseph Jenkins Roberts, and other members of
the proadministration group remained in control during
the transition to republic status in 1847. Although the opposition party apparently concurred in the decision of
1847 to break the ties binding the settlers to the American
Colonization Society, it vigorously opposed the ratification
of the proposed constitution and threatened to have Grand
Bassa secede from the new state.[4]

The True Liberian, or Republican, Party founded by

[4] Huberich, *op. cit.*, I, 670, 728–729, 841–842.

President Roberts and his followers after independence retained control of the national government until the election of 1869. The Anti-Administration Party, which
rallied under the banner of Samuel Benedict in opposition
to ratification of the constitution in 1847, never seriously
threatened the Republicans. Although the Anti-Administration Party did not constitute a serious opponent, divisions arose within the Republican Party itself regarding
the alleged domination by Monrovia and Montserrado
County of the rest of the country. Curiously enough, the
most divisive issue within the Republican Party concerned
racial extraction. Roberts, an octoroon, was rejected in his
bid for a fifth term in 1855 in favor of Stephen A. Benson.
The latter was also of mixed ancestry, but he was considerably darker in complexion than Roberts. Benson had the
support of the poorer Americo-Liberians and the Congoes,
who, as noted in Chapter 1, were the descendants of
Congolese, Nigerian, and other Africans who had been
taken from slaving vessels intercepted en route to the New
World. Both the lower-class settlers and the Congoes felt
discriminated against by those of "brighter" skin color.[5]
By the election of 1869, the issues of skin pigmentation
and ancestry split the solidarity of the Republican ranks
and brought to power the True Whig Party, which had
been formed to oppose the lighter-skinned aristocracy. The
candidate of the True Whigs, Edward J. Roye, was Liberia's first full-blooded Negro President. His birth in
America, his superior education, and his meteoric rise in
Liberian commerce, as well as his distinguished service on
the Supreme Court, made him sufficiently acceptable to
the Republicans to bring about a peaceful transfer of party
control.

[5] Frederick Starr, *Liberia* (Chicago, 1913), p. 90.

Roye, however, was a tragic figure. His personal involvement in the disastrous British loan of 1871 and his attempt that year to extend the term of office from two to four years led to his ouster and to his subsequent death under mysterious circumstances. Whether he was executed or died escaping to a British vessel remains a matter of legend. A Republican junta forced his Vice-President, James S. Smith, to accept a truncated term of office and brought ex-President Roberts back to the presidency. The Republicans were victorious in the next two elections, but in 1877 came the first of a series of Whig victories that has continued unbroken into the present period. Whig domination was not really assured, however, until the election in 1883 of Hilary R. W. Johnson, Liberia's first "son of the soil" President. Johnson, who had the nomination of both the True Whig and the Republican parties, declared himself a Whig after the election.

Thus, during the nineteenth century Liberia arrived at the pattern of one-party rule that today has become the political norm in the newly independent states of Africa. From 1869 to 1883 was the only period of intensive interparty competition in Liberia during which the opposition had more than merely a theoretical chance of unseating the ruling party. Thereafter, Americo-Liberians found themselves captives of the very situation they had created by the expansion of the Republic into the hostile tribal hinterland beyond the coastal countries and the subsequent conflicts with the British and French, who were coveting the same inland areas. The need for solidarity in meeting the threats of tribal rebellion and European occupation convinced the Americo-Liberian leadership of the value of the single-party system. Periodically, incidents such as the Kru uprising during the First World War or the League of Nations inquiry regarding charges of slavery in Liberia during the early 1930's have reinforced the Americo-Liberian faith in the wisdom of this decision. When pressed to the wall, the party leadership has made tactical retreats and jettisoned its standard-bearer, as it did with President William D. Coleman in 1900 and again with President Charles D. B. King and Vice-President Allen N. Yancy in 1930. The strategy of using the True Whig Party as the vehicle of Americo-Liberian supremacy, however, has remained intact.

CHAPTER 4

A "New Deal" for
the Hinterland

The pacification of the tribal people through coercion or the seduction of its leadership and the emergence of a single-party system were fairly effective in maintaining Americo-Liberian control over Liberia during most of the nineteenth century and well into the twentieth. In the 1950's however, with nationalist independence movements threatening to dislodge Europeans from their dominant positions in neighboring states, it became apparent that more positive measures were required to secure the tribal people's acceptance of the legitimacy of Americo-Liberian rule. Indeed, three decades before Kwame Nkrumah's Convention Peoples Party of Ghana succeeded a colonial regime in the Gold Coast, the storm clouds of discontent among the Liberian tribal people had already gathered. The crisis that had been brewing during the administration of President Charles D. B. King (1920–1930) gave the settler elite clear warning that their control of the tribal majority was being seriously challenged.

The League of Nations Crisis

The crisis of 1930 confronted the Americo-Liberian elite with the gravest threat since the days of early settlement. Not only was there a brief recurrence of tribal rebellion along the Kru Coast, but the factor of external intervention was compounded far beyond the previous meddling of Liberia's colonial neighbors, Britain and France. This time the European menace was supported by the League of Nations. Moreover, the United States under President Herbert Hoover dramatically reversed two American policies. First of all, the U.S. government publicly rebuked the Liberian government, whose cause it normally championed against the colonial powers. Secondly, the United States indicated a willingness to cooperate with the League, which it had helped create but had refused to join.[1]

The crisis of 1930 was in part a reaction to the increasing effectiveness of the elite in bringing the interior under military and administrative control and in collecting the hut tax. Most of the antagonism, however, centered upon labor practices, an area in which the Americo-Liberians were not the only offenders. Both chiefs and influential Americo-Liberians had been involved in the abuses of the traditional pawning system whereby an impoverished tribal person could indenture himself or a relative until a debt had been repaid. In traditional society there were many safeguards for the system, but these had been weakened under the imposition of Americo-Liberian rule and the open collaboration of Americo-Liberian officials and tribal chiefs. There had been instances, for example, of pawns remaining unredeemed for forty years or more. Pawning, incidentally, was a fairly common practice throughout West Africa. One of the ironies of the League

[1] For an excellent background discussion of the crisis, see Raymond L. Buell, *Liberia: A Century of Survival, 1847–1947* in University of Pennsylvania Museum, *African Handbook,* No. 7 (Philadelphia: University of Pennsylvania Press, 1947).

controversy was that the British government, which so sanctimoniously criticized the pawning system in Liberia, had only in 1928 overcome the resistance of chiefs and abolished the last form of domestic slavery in neighboring Sierra Leone.

Some of the labor discontent was a direct reaction to government practices. There had been much abuse of the porterage system, under which Liberian officials could conscript able-bodied men to help carry them (in hammocks) and their supplies while on tour in the district. The requests for porters as well as the recruitment of both males and females for unpaid labor on roads and other public projects frequently came at the peak of the planting or harvesting seasons. The treatment of laborers on these projects by unsupervised gang foremen was apparently quite ruthless.

The most serious charges, however, concerned the forcible recruitment of labor to serve on private projects. Reference has already been made to the illegal use of native farm labor, recruited by chiefs, for work on the farms of the district commissioners and other prominent Americo-Liberians. The signing of the agreement with the Firestone Plantations Company in 1926 aggravated this situation. The officers of Firestone acknowledged that, at least during the early years of their effort to produce rubber in Liberia, chiefs had assisted in the recruitment of involuntary labor.[2] What aroused the international commu-

[2] For some interesting comments on labor recruitment practices in the 1960's, see the interviews reported in Robert W. Clower, George Dalton, Mitchell Harwitz, and A. A. Walters, *Growth without Development: An Economic Survey of Liberia* (Evanston, Ill.: Northwestern University Press, 1966), pp. 296–298.

nity, however, were the midnight raids on tribal villages by Liberian soldiers seeking laborers for the cocoa and other plantations on the Spanish island of Fernando Po. What made the forcible recruitment particularly obnoxious was the active or at least tacit approval of many high Liberian officials, including Vice President Allen Yancy. It was even charged, but not definitely substantiated, that President King himself was involved in the lucrative enterprise, which brought $45 a head for each of 3,000 men exported and a bonus of $5,000 for every additional group of 1,500 recruited.

The plight of the tribal people gained international attention during a 1927 tour in the United States by Thomas J. R. Faulkner, who had been unsuccessful that year in his electoral bid to replace Mr. King. The American press, and ultimately the State Department, accepted Faulkner's charges regarding the King administration's role in condoning slavery, corruption, and "primitive" customs. In 1929, following a protest note by the U.S. State Department, Liberia agreed to request an international commission of inquiry to look into the charges. The Council of the League of Nations appointed a tripartite commission consisting of representatives from the United States, Great Britain, and Liberia, and headed by Dr. Cuthbert Christy, a physician with many years' experience in West Africa. The Christy Commission substantiated in 1930 many of the charges regarding the pawning system, the abuses of compulsory labor, the forcible recruitment of laborers for Fernando Po, and the complicity of Vice-President Yancy and other high Liberian officials. They did not, however, find outright slavery in Liberia, at least as defined in the Anti-Slavery Convention of 1925. Parenthetically, it might be noted that the Commission did not acknowledge that many of the practices criticized in Liberia were prevalent—in some instances even more flagrant—in certain European dependencies in Africa.

President King attempted to respond to the popular criticism as well as to the Christy Commission's findings by banning the exportation of labor and the pawning system and by outlawing slavery. This tacit admission of Liberian guilt, however, so outraged many leading Americo-Liberians that both President King and Vice-President Yancy were compelled to resign in December, 1930, with Secretary of State Edwin Barclay assuming the presidency. This by no means ended the controversy. During the next four years a number of plans and counterplans were exchanged by the League, the Liberian leaders, and the British and American governments. Firestone also participated in the international discussions, much to its embarrassment. The most severe proposal came in 1932 as a result of the inquiry the preceding year by the Brunot Committee of the League, named for its chairman, a former French colonial governor. The Brunot proposal would have placed the fiscal and legal affairs of the Republic as well as its administration of the hinterland under an international supervisor. The refusal of the Liberian government to accept the proposal without amendment prolonged the discussions, and eventually the diplomatic delaying tactics paid off. An improvement in its economic situation through a rise in the price of rubber and the more friendly attitude of the administration of Franklin D. Roosevelt permitted the controversy to come to an inconclusive end in 1935, when American and Liberian diplomatic relations, which had been broken in 1930, were resumed.

President Barclay's efforts to reorganize the administrative service in the hinterland and to introduce a public health service and other programs of benefit to the tribal people were applauded by the international community. But the Barclay reform measures were to a great extent undermined by the obsession of certain Whig leaders with the desire to punish Americo-Liberians and tribal people who had given testimony to the various League commissions. The ruthless suppression of the unrest along the Kru Coast brought outward stability but undying hostility on the part of many tribal persons toward the Americo-Liberian leadership. Rumors of revolutionary activity cropped up repeatedly, and many individuals, including a recent Secretary of Public Instruction, the late Nathaniel Massaquoi, were tried and imprisoned during the grim Barclay days for allegedly attempting to overthrow the Americo-Liberian ruling class by force.

The Election of President Tubman

The election of President Tubman in 1943 signaled a change in the spirit as well as the substance of the relationship between the tribal people and the descendants of the settlers. Although Tubman's credentials among the Americo-Liberian elite were of the highest order, and although he was Barclay's personal choice as his successor, it was obvious from the outset that he intended to be an independent political commander. In addition to a very dynamic personality, he had a remarkable familiarity with the intricacies of the Liberian political system, which he learned from his father, who eventually became Speaker of the House of Representatives. Even more significant, however, was the highly intimate knowledge he had gained of the political system as a legal defender of the Liberian officials involved in the League of Nations inquiry into the Fernando Po scandals. Secondly, he had developed an independent base of political power among both tribal people and the lower-class Americo-Liberians which permitted him to be something other than a mere defender of the traditional relationship between the Whig aristocracy and the tribal people. By the time he became a candidate for the presidency, he had developed a considerable reputation as an eloquent lawyer who often took the cases of penniless clients even against prominent Americo-Liberian adversaries. For this reason, the latter should not have been too surprised by the liberal posture assumed by the man who took office on January 1, 1944. The Old Guard had assumed that Tubman—like most of his predecessors— would ignore the fiery campaign rhetoric of reform once he had the reins of office firmly in hand. How mistaken they were!

The Open-Door Policy

Among the first of Tubman's programs to alter affairs in the tribal hinterland was the Open-Door Policy. This policy acknowledged that the previous attempt to isolate the people of the hinterland from external economic influences and insulate them against modernity was unrealistic. There was the danger, too, that a further delay in the exposure of the tribal people to the twentieth century would build a time bomb under the archaic political, social, and economic structure that the descendants of the settlers had inherited. Economic development, instead of undermining Americo-Liberian control of the Republic, might finance more modern and efficient means of control. While recognizing the potential dangers of exposing the tribal people to Westernization, industrialization, and urbanization, the Old Guard accepted Tubman's arguments that social change could be controlled: change would be evolutionary rather than revolutionary.

The controlled change was to take place by opening Liberia to massive foreign investment and exploitation of its agricultural and mineral resources. Tubman had enacted laws at the outset of his presidency that gave foreign investors full freedom of entry and repatriation of their capital and profits. This legislation imposed few restrictions upon corporate structure or regulations regarding employment policies and practices. As a consequence, from an economy that in 1945 was dependent largely upon one enterprise—Firestone—Liberia in the next two decades attracted forty major foreign concessionaires and countless smaller ones. From almost total dependence upon rubber in 1945, the exploitation of its vast iron resources gave Liberia an additional source of wealth whose export value has steadily risen. By 1966 the export value of iron ore was three times that of rubber ($112,000,000 to $30,000,000).

The diversification of the sources of foreign investment and personnel gave the Americo-Liberian leadership greater latitude in its foreign and domestic policies. It would not be under the thumb of any single alien power. Moreover, the increased revenues from the foreign exploitation of Liberia's resources gave the government the funds to build a more effective road system, modernize its army and police force, and control the processes of social, economic, and political change.

While Tubman's Open-Door Policy may have been advanced as a means for buttressing continued Americo-Liberian domination within the Republic, it must be recognized that development has in fact brought positive benefits to many tribal areas where the inhabitants had previously known government officials only as collectors of taxes and recruiters of labor. Roads, bridges, and other public works have done much to bring the people of the hinterland into contact with each other and with the Americo-Liberians of the coast. New roads have made it possible for teachers, medical technicians, agricultural instructors, and others to reach the vast interior of Liberia, where the majority of the people live. Roads have also permitted a more rapid exploitation of the natural resources of the interior. With this development has come a radical transformation in the way of life of tribesmen, who until recently were rigidly wedded to subsistence economies and able to afford few of the material luxuries of Westernization.

Extension of Suffrage and Representation

The second plank in Tubman's program of reform was the extension of legislative representation and suffrage to the tribal majority. Recalling that the granting of Liberian citizenship to the tribal people at the turn of the century had cost the Americo-Liberians nothing in terms of real power (but had been notably successful in forestalling British encroachments along the northwestern frontier), the Tubman regime has attempted to eliminate many of the formal legal barriers to participation by the tribal element in the affairs of the Republic. A property qualification for voting remains, but it has been revised downward to extend the ballot to the owner of any hut upon which taxes have been paid. Suffrage, moreover, is now an individual right in contrast to the past, when a chief, acting in his corporate capacity as the holder of title to tribal land, could register and vote the members of his community as a unit.[3] Further, during Tubman's administration the vote has been extended to women.

Along with the changes in suffrage qualifications, the form of representation for the tribal people has been altered. In the past any tribe that paid one hundred dollars had the privilege of electing one of its members as a delegate to the House of Representatives. There he had the opportunity to discuss and vote upon all matters relating to tribal interests. In 1944 the regular membership of the House of Representatives was increased to permit the hinterland areas as well as the tribal areas within the five coastal counties to have regular representation. This process was brought to its logical culmination in 1964 with the elimination of the provincial system of administration and the creation of four new counties in the interior, each of which elects two Senators to the upper house of the Liberian Legislature. Finally, at the executive and judicial levels as well, Tubman has publicized the appointment of persons with tribal backgrounds to positions of prominence.

The Unification Program

The keystone of the Tubman program to bridge the chasm separating the Americo-Liberian minority from the tribal majority has been the Unification Policy. More important than any particular act of legislation or executive decree, the Unification Policy represents a creative posture that permits the tribal people to identify with the

[3] George G. Parker, "Acculturation in Liberia" (Ph.D. thesis, Kennedy School of Missions, Hartford Seminary, 1944), p. 261.

Liberian nation through the personality of the President. Under Tubman's administration, for the first time in Liberian history the doors of the Executive Mansion have been open to tribal persons who had suggestions or petitions of grievance to present to the President. Moreover, he has developed in a more systematic fashion the device of personal diplomacy in the hinterland initiated in a most sporadic fashion by President King.

Tubman has made it a point to visit each of the main headquarters in the interior during a three-year period. There he holds extended sessions of his Executive Council in which the people and chiefs seek correction of wrongs, request new programs in health or education, secure executive arbitration of boundary disputes, and in other ways solicit the help of the President. Without being burdened by legal restrictions or bound by precedents, the President has meted out a form of substantive justice which has had a tremendous impact upon the tribal people, most of whom had long felt isolated from Liberian politics and had never had the opportunity of seeing a Liberian President. The summary dismissal of errant district commissioners (including a very close relative of the President), the immediate granting of justice, and the promises to extend the benefits of the new economic development to the hinterland have been significant factors in almost eliminating the incidence of violent opposition on the part of tribal people to Americo-Liberian rule. Tubman's Executive Council decisions, moreover, have frequently struck at one of the most tender spots in the relationship between the two elements, namely, the illegal acquisition of land in the interior by leading members of the Americo-Liberian community. The fines, public rebuke, forfeiture of crops, and other stern treatment accorded the latter at the Salala Executive Council in 1945 did much to reassure the tribal people that their traditional land tenure rights would be respected.

There have been other ways, too, in which Tubman has attempted to eradicate the distinctions between the members of the two communities and to indicate that the tribal people have a right to be proud of their traditional heritage. The President often appears in tribal dress on civic occasions, has taken a series of tribal names, and has encouraged the appreciation of native dancing and art forms. The employment of anthropologists to study tribal customs, law, and social organization is also evidence of a new appreciation of the indigenous culture of the Liberian masses.

Perhaps the most promising sign in the entire picture is the sense of guilt that Americo-Liberians now have when it comes to differentiating in public speeches and writings between themselves and the tribal element. The dropping of the term "Americo-Liberian" and the employing of ambiguous expressions such as "the natives and the other element" or the "civilized people and the other element" constitute evidence that the self-assuredness of the settler aristocracy has been undermined. Moreover, frontal attacks on the early settlers have been made by prominent members of the Americo-Liberian community. During the commencement address at Bromley School for Girls in 1960, the sister of an important cabinet official referred to the founding fathers of Liberia as the "ill-prepared, ill-informed, and illegitimate offspring of the union between master and slave." Since Tubman came to power, it has once again become respectable for someone named Caine to call himself Kandakai and a Freeman to resort to the tribal form of Fahnbulleh. This has been very important for Liberian students abroad and for others attempting to emphasize their ties with Africa rather than the West. Thus, County Superintendent George F. Sherman became G. Flama Sherman upon his appointment as Ambassador to Ghana.

The Sources of Change

The roots of Tubman's Unification Policy are various, and it would be grossly unfair to attribute the change solely to a desire on the part of the Americo-Liberian elite to insulate itself from the wave of nationalism undermining alien rule in other parts of Africa. Many Liberians had traveled to Europe, America, and other African territories and returned convinced that the lot of the tribal people should be improved. Many in the upper class had familial and other personal ties with tribal communities and were sufficiently indignant about tribal discrimination to advocate reform long before Tubman arrived on the scene. Nevertheless, it was clear that the nationalist unrest mounting elsewhere would one day touch Liberia; if the settler element did not lead the tribal people to modernity and grant them political and social rights, the latter would one day try to achieve these things on their own. Thus, if the Americo-Liberians could not prevent change, they could at least attempt to control it.

What forces made change inevitable? Certainly the events of World War II and in particular the presence of over five thousand American troops, both white and black, had a marked impact upon the tribal people and the poorer element within the Americo-Liberian community.

The free spending as well as the free living of the American troops had a disruptive effect upon the Liberian economy and tribal social codes, but the presence of the Americans also drove home the idea that a life of poverty need not be accepted blindly. Moreover, ideas of a political and social character inevitably emerged from this new cultural contact.

Economic development, which had really been launched in the 1920's when Firestone Plantations Company took over the operation of the abandoned rubber plantations near Monrovia, has had a more sustained impact in breaking down traditional tribal relationships and in creating economic demands that would eventually need political solutions. Firestone punctured the myth of the lack of economic motivation on the part of the Liberian tribesmen, and the myth was dealt its death blow by the iron ore companies and other foreign concessions brought into Liberia by Tubman's Open-Door Policy in the postwar period. The tribesman has taken readily to a money economy and to the new status that material wealth can bring to one in his tribal area as well as in the new urban centers. The influx of foreigners under the Open-Door Policy has also exposed the tribal people to individuals from several continents and reversed the long-standing attempt by the Americo-Liberians to insulate the tribal people against alien influences.

Another sustained contributor to social change has been the education of tribal youth, a responsibility assumed almost entirely by the Christian missionaries prior to the Tubman administration. Education has produced a corps of tribal youths who no longer are satisfied with a second-class status in their own country. As will be noted in the following chapter, higher education either at the University of Liberia or through foreign scholarships has been the virtual monopoly of the Americo-Liberian class. The first significant break for the tribal people came in the period following World War II when the Episcopal Church, with the assistance of the Methodist and Lutheran missions, established Cuttington College. The institution has been more practical in its orientation and more insistent upon maintaining high academic standards than has the University of Liberia. Since Cuttington is located at Gbarnga, over a hundred miles into the interior, it has long been regarded as a "bush" college by the Americo-Liberian youth, who has preferred the political and social activity of Monrovia.

The development of radio and the press have not been as significant instigators of change in Liberia as in other parts of Africa, and in a sense the government is missing a significant opportunity for the political indoctrination of the tribal masses by not having a strong AM radio station under government control. The national broadcasting station (ELBC) in Monrovia can only be heard in pockets of the country under the best of atmospheric conditions unless one has a very expensive set. The inexpensive transistor radios that are being widely distributed throughout the country do pick up the Voice of America (which has a transmitter outside Monrovia) and the English and tribal language programs of ELWA, the Sudan Interior Mission radio station in Monrovia. In certain sectors of the country, however, it is easier to pick up broadcasts from Guinea or Radio Peking than it is to receive Western interpretations of the news.

A much older and more effective means of communica-

tions remains of course: the carrying of news by the steady
flow of people moving back and forth across the artificial
boundaries separating Liberia from Guinea, Sierra Leone,
and the Ivory Coast. The efforts of Sékou Touré in
Guinea and Félix Houphouët-Boigny in the Ivory Coast
to organize mass-based parties have not gone unnoticed by
the tribal people of Liberia. Of even greater significance to
the Americo-Liberians is the chain of events in Sierra
Leone that has brought the tribal people to political
power. There the Creoles, who as descendants of British-
released slaves have roots similar to the Americo-Liberians,
have had to accommodate themselves to a minority political role within the newly independent state.

The success of President Tubman's Unification Policy
in changing conditions in the hinterland and in changing
tribal attitudes toward the Liberian political system is best
underscored by the very real personal popularity that
Tubman seems to enjoy wherever he journeys in the interior. Nevertheless, a group of leading True Whigs only
a few years ago acknowledged quite frankly that "the lines
of cleavage are beginning to lessen somewhat, but the distinctions still remain. . . . It would be inaccurate to say
that at this time members of the tribal groups are not at a
disadvantage. . . ." [4]

[4] John P. Mitchell, ed., United Christian Fellowship Conference of
Liberia, *Changing Liberia: A Challenge to the Christian* (Switzerland, 1959), p. 17. The Conference included among others the Secretary of the Treasury Charles Sherman and Doris Banks Henries, the
wife of the Speaker of the House. Mitchell later became Secretary of
Education.

Formalism and Reform

Undoubtedly the policies and personal magnetism of President Tubman have done much to convince the tribal people that not all Americo-Liberians are exploiters. It is perhaps equally apparent to young and old alike among the Loma, Kpelle, and other people of the interior that Tubman does not represent the entire Whig community. The Americo-Liberian settlers and their descendants survived for a century and a quarter before Tubman's assumption of office, and the Old Guard at least was not about to surrender tried and accepted techniques of survival without a struggle. Where they have not frontally attacked the President and his policies, the more conservative Americo-Liberians have accepted the rhetoric of reform without feeling obliged to give it substance. Indeed, in this respect the opponents of change are continuing the tendency towards *formalism,* a dominant characteristic of Liberian politics almost from the outset. It is against this background of formalism as a political philosophy and as a way of life that one must attempt to evaluate the reality of reform under the Tubman regime.

The tendency toward formalism is readily apparent in the constant emphasis upon constitutionalism, adherence to legal technicalities in the courts, and the charade of conducting elaborate electoral campaigns when there are no opponents to the True Whig Party candidates. The emphasis upon proper form and procedure, indeed, pervades almost all aspects of social intercourse in Liberia. The tendency to emphasize form and style at the expense of substance, moreover, is not limited to the upper strata of the Americo-Liberian community; it infects the poorer element of that society as well as the tribal person who has only recently migrated to Monrovia. A casual and impatient visitor to Liberia frequently fails to comprehend or appreciate the rigorous attention to detail regarding dress and other items of protocol on state occasions, the exacting fashion in which a preacher adheres to the Order of Worship in a church service, and the almost stylized ritual that must be observed in completing a transaction with a trader or in circumventing a demand for a "dash" on the part of a traffic policeman. A hinterland court clerk will take great pains to make an exact transcript of a case without any attention being given to the matter of keeping, let alone compiling, the records in any systematic way so that they could constitute a guide for the more efficient administration of a district.[5] The act of making a record has a logic and mystique of its own almost unrelated to improving government procedures. The historical basis for this emphasis upon formalism may perhaps be that Liberia was founded by men and women who were in, but not part of, an antebellum Southern society in America where the propriety of an act was given great value.

Formalism is highly evident in the political sphere. Campaign rhetoric, letters to the editor, church sermons, and debates in the Legislature are replete with demands that politicians must observe both the letter and the spirit of the Constitution of 1847.[6] It matters little that the elaborate description in the Liberian Constitution of the ways

[5] *Africa Report,* XII (May, 1967), 52.

[6] The basic Constitution was drafted by Professor Simon Greenleaf of Harvard University. Its description of the structures of government, the distribution of powers, and the Bill of Rights is modeled after the United States Constitution of 1787, as amended.

in which power is distributed among a President, a bi-
cameral Legislature, and a Supreme Court bears even less
resemblance to the actual distribution of power than it
does in most other societies with written constitutions.
The absence until recently of a collected code of laws or a
compilation of Supreme Court decisions, moreover, has
not prevented Americo-Liberian lawyers from arguing elo-
quently and at great length about the fine points of law
and legal precedents. In the management of local affairs,
moreover, prominent families in each of the counties and
the urbanized communities have a considerable degree of
autonomy despite the explicit absence of a federal division
of authority and the absence of meaningful structures of
local government. Yet, the formalities of centralized control over the administration of national programs are rigorously adhered to.

While we cannot dismiss the formal structures of government and the formal allocations of authority as unim-
portant, we must appreciate that they have relevance
largely to the problem of legitimacy of the existing leadership group. Despite the fact that Tubman in 1967 had no
opponent in his bid for a sixth term of office, he was required to go through the formality of campaigning. Earlier
in his career, no one doubted that he could continue in
office indefinitely even though the Constitution had been
amended specifically to prevent the President from serving
more than one eight-year term. Despite its obvious violation of the spirit of the Constitution, Tubman felt obliged
to have the Constitution formally amended so that he
could succeed himself. I have dealt with the problems of
formalism at length in order to stress the fact that the constant revision of suffrage requirements, the extension of

the principle of representation, and the changes in the administrative framework of the national government have not brought about an actual realignment of power. The old French proverb about "the more things change, the more they remain the same" is certainly applicable to much of the reform that has taken place in Liberia during the past quarter of a century. What is important are the mechanisms devised by the Americo-Liberian elite for ensuring that the changes in the Liberian political system will be evolutionary rather than revolutionary in character. Although a façade of mass participation in the political process is being presented to the outside world, the decision-making process within the True Whig Party remains firmly under the control of the Americo-Liberian minority.

In the subsequent chapters on the primacy of politics, the organization of the True Whig Party, and the continuing strength of family ties among the Americo-Liberian community, I shall attempt to demonstrate the mechanisms whereby the basic distribution of political authority of the pre-Tubman era has remained dominant while at the same time a wide measure of change has taken place within the economy, the educational system, and other structures of Liberian Society.

CHAPTER 5

Politics Is King

One of the critical factors in maintaining Americo-Liberian control over the processes of change in the new Liberia is the priority given to politics at the expense of other kinds of social interaction.[1] Exceptions obviously exist, for no political system is water-tight, but a Liberian today rarely can enjoy great prestige or pursue his professional goals without some political base. An individual enjoys a position of influence in a church, a business, a charitable organization, or a fraternal society because he holds, or has held, office in the Liberian government or the True Whig Party. Prominence in a nonpolitical structure, then, is a reward for excellent performance in the political arena. The monopoly of the political leadership over religious, economic, and other institutions guarantees that these structures will not fall under the sway of those not committed to the preservation of the existing distribution of political power. Anyone who attempts to gain a position of influence in society without first gaining political sanction is regarded with suspicion.

The consequences for the rapid modernization of the

[1] Sections of this chapter have appeared previously in my article on Liberia in James S. Coleman and Carl G. Rosberg, eds., *Political Parties and National Integration in Tropical Africa* (Berkeley: University of California Press, 1964), pp. 448–481. I am indebted to the University of California Press for its permission to republish sections of that study here.

Liberian society are depressing. The independent, nonpolitical entrepreneur simply does not survive. He is either
crushed by a series of legal or illegal barriers, or he "gets
into line." In conforming to the norms of administrative
behavior peculiar to Liberia, the young Western-educated
Liberian soon finds his professional ethics and his textbook
skills shelved and his reforming zeal diminished as he attempts to navigate the intricate political maze and learn
the expediencies necessary for occupational survival. The
fruits of cooperation soon make the reforming zealot a defender of the *status quo*. He develops in time the politically sensitive antennae of his seniors and helps perpetuate
a situation that makes the Liberian political system a modern equivalent of a Renaissance Italian city-state.

Economic Structures

TRIBAL INVOLVEMENT

The Americo-Liberian elite displays an ambivalent attitude toward the involvement of tribal people in economic
associations. Certain traditional work societies, such as the
kuus among the Mano and Kpelle of the interior, have
been permitted to flourish.[2] The government is equally
indulgent with respect to the thrift, improvement, and
burial associations so popular among the Bassa, Kru, and
other tribal people who have gravitated to Monrovia and
other urbanized centers. The limited economic and social
objectives of these groupings have been rigidly maintained
by the government-appointed leaders who regulate the
conduct of their fellow tribesmen in the urban areas. Also
controlled by the urban tribal leaders are the nativistic re-

[2] See Blanchard, *op. cit.*

ligious societies, such as the Bassa Community Church, which could challenge the orthodox Christian leadership of Liberia.

The involvement of tribal people in more modern forms of economic associations, on the other hand, is viewed with open hostility by the Whig leadership. Aware of the role that the cocoa cooperatives of Ghana and the coffee cooperatives of Tanganyika played in the rise of nationalist movements, this writer was not surprised to hear President Tubman indicate that the people of Liberia were not yet ready for cooperative societies. In the absence of government support of cooperatives, the cash-crop economy for some time to come seems destined to remain under the control of foreign entrepreneurs and leaders of the Americo-Liberian class, with little competition from peasant cultivators. The animosity apparently even extends to the recently urbanized tribal person who attempts to involve himself in the money economy by "making small store": establishing himself as a sidewalk peddler. In 1967, President Tubman took action against the Lebanese traders who were supplying these small entrepreneurs with their razor blades, shoelaces, and chewing gum. Apparently the Lebanese found themselves in competition with Liberian officials who wanted to monopolize petty trading.

TRADE UNIONISM

Superficially at least, the tribal people of Liberia have made some progress in at least one sector of the economy. Since 1949, a year after Liberia signed the international treaty regulating Freedom of Association and Protection of the Right to Organize, trade unions have operated in Liberia with assistance and encouragement from United

States and Western European labor organizations. The government passed a Labor Code, and from time to time President Tubman has gone on record expressing the government's support of collective bargaining, encouragement of an "active and free labor organization," and improvement in the conditions of labor in the agricultural, mining, and transport sectors of the Liberian economy.

How does one account for government encouragement of structures that can be—and indeed with increasing frequency have been—used to challenge the existing power distribution in Liberia? The answer lies largely in the Whig leadership's concern with its external image. Painfully aware that abuse of Liberian tribal labor brought about external intervention and toppled a government in the 1930's, the Tubman regime has attempted to avoid criticism by the ILO (International Labor Organization) and by the leaders of the American labor movement in particular. One of Tubman's cardinal techniques for survival is the neutralization of a potentially hostile international environment.

Thus, the Liberian government has not opposed unions *per se;* they have opposed only *effective* unions. One device for keeping unions ineffective has been control of their leadership. The two major unions in the industrial sector have been the Labor Congress of Liberia and the CIO (Congress of Industrial Organizations).[3] The former has long been under the control of T. Dupigny-Leigh, a member of the House of Representatives and formerly Tubman's social secretary. Dupigny-Leigh a few years ago stated that he did "not favor strikes." The larger organization, the CIO, during much of the period since 1960 was under the leadership of William V. S. Tubman, Jr. The

[3] Assisted by, but not formally affiliated with, the American CIO.

President's son has also been in charge of labor and public relations for LAMCO (Liberian American-Swedish Minerals Company). He thus was able to use his leadership talents to work both sides of several streets. The major union in the agricultural sector, the Firestone Rubber Tappers Association, was formed only after a severe strike in 1966, and its officers have either been selected by Firestone or elected under company supervision. Moreover to prevent the possible consolidation of union power, the government in 1966 specifically forbade the formation of unions that would represent the interests of both agricultural and industrial workers.

In addition to controlling the leadership and organizational structure of unions in Liberia, the government has pulled their teeth by outlawing their ultimate weapons: strikes and boycotts. Prior to the enactment of the Labor Code in 1963, all strikes were illegal until the dispute over wages or conditions of labor had been submitted to a labor court. Inasmuch as no labor court had ever been established, all strikes have been in fact illegal. The subsequent requirement that no strike could be called without a decision by the government-established Labor Practices Review Board has also frustrated union leadership. The Board during the past few years has been criticized by the ILO for either failing to meet when faced with a strike threat, failing to issue a decision, or unreasonably delaying the announcement of its decision. Even when the Board decides in favor of the workers, there seems to be no means for enforcing a judgment against a company.[4]

Legal or not, strikes by both organized and unorganized

[4] "Complaints Presented by the I.C.F.T.U., the I.F.P.A.A.W., and the M.I.F. against the Government of Liberia," Case 506, International Labor Office, *Official Bulletin,* L, no. 3 (July, 1967).

laborers have been, in fact, increasingly frequent since 1961. The spate of a dozen or more strikes in 1961 alone almost equaled those for the entire period from 1949 to 1960. The general strike of September, 1961, occurred shortly after Tubman's son had gone abroad on his honeymoon. It set the pattern of unorganized violence on the part of workers, followed by the use of government troops against strikers, the arrest of the union leaders on charges of sedition, and the charges of "foreign" conspiracy that was repeated in 1963 and again in 1966. In 1966 major strikes occurred not only at the Firestone but also the Goodrich rubber plantations and at the LAMCO iron mining operations at Nimba. Coming as they did, in conjunction with military coups in Nigeria and Ghana, the strikes prompted the government to give the President emergency powers to deal with unions and strikes, to mobilize for defense, and to take other extraordinary measures. Clearly, the Whig leadership was beginning to fear the creature it had had to spawn, and its actions in dealing with the striking unions indeed brought on the very international criticism by the ILO it had hoped to avoid by fostering unions in the first place.

COMMERCE AND THE AMERICO-LIBERIAN

The circumspect posture of the Whig leadership extends even to economic associations whose membership is limited largely to Americo-Liberians. In part, however, the explanation for the failure of the Americo-Liberians to involve themselves in major economic undertakings is historical. The disdain of the upper ranks of the Americo-Liberian community toward commerce and industry has almost universally been commented upon by observers of the Liberian scene since the middle of the last century. Much of it can be accounted for as responses to the paternalism of the American Colonization Society, the attitudes against commerce imparted by some of the radical missionary groups, the economic depressions that wiped out hard-earned savings, and the emphasis that the defense of the Republic against the Europeans placed upon legal and political education.[5] It can also be explained in terms of the inevitable politics of a small state. The system permits the political leadership to control the economy to its personal advantage through its manipulation of tariffs, the granting of franchises and subsidies, and the letting of contracts. The rule for the ambitious businessman is to follow Nkrumah's advice: "Seek ye first the political kingdom." The marked failure, for example, of the Liberian National Businessmen's Association to constitute an effective force in Liberian politics is all the more curious when viewed against the remarkable economic developments taking place in the country today. The fact is that few Liberians prefer, or are permitted, to become wealthy by direct involvement in the management of agricultural, industrial, or commercial enterprises. If they reap the benefits of the current economic development, they do so as a by-product of their involvement in the affairs of the True Whig Party. This is not new. The high value placed upon politics by the Americo-Liberian elite has been recorded by many previous observers of the Liberian scene. Professor Frederick Starr in 1913, for example, wrote: "In Liberia there is a general desire to feed at the public trough; it makes no difference what a man is or what he has accomplished,

[5] George W. Ellis, "Political Institutions in Liberia," *American Political Science Review,* V (1911), p. 216.

every one is ready to go into politics; neither trade, agriculture, nor professional life restrains a man who has political opportunities presented to him; everybody of ability wants office." [6]

Whatever the causes of the preference for politics over business, it is apparent that the attitude helps maintain Whig political solidarity. Instead of using his economic position as a base from which to make particularistic demands upon the political system, an Americo-Liberian leader exploits his political position to gain a greater share in the productivity of the economy. He becomes a politician first and a businessman second. An Americo-Liberian who attempts to reverse the procedure or tries to remain entirely aloof from the political system is usually doomed to failure. The maverick can invariably be driven out of business or coerced into conformity by a series of devices: the refusal of the government to grant a visa or an export license, the harassing visit of a government auditor, or the strict enforcement of a long-dormant tax law. The obvious antipathy of the government toward both Americo-Liberian and tribal businessmen was acknowledged by several officials, who publicly agreed that as a "rule the government does not do business with Liberian businessmen." [7] More accurately, the government does not do business with *independent-minded* businessmen.

An analysis the author did of 386 companies registered in Montserrado County revealed that only 63 were owned by either Americo-Liberians or tribal persons. The Liberian concerns fell into two categories: a petty business, such as a florist shop, bar, gift shop, hostel, or barbershop,

[6] *Op. cit.,* pp. 210–211.
[7] Mitchell, *op. cit.,* p. 51.

run by a small entrepreneur who lacked real political stature; or a series of major firms owned—but not managed—by officials such as the Secretary of Commerce, the Undersecretary for Agriculture, the former Secretary of State and Adviser to the President on Foreign Affairs, and several members of the Legislature. Moreover, of the firms largely financed by Swiss, Swedish, and other European investors, the more successful ones included prominent Liberian officials on their boards of directors or retained lawyer-legislators to represent them in their negotiations with the government. One of the Liberian officials most deeply involved in the so-called private sector of the economy in 1961 was Stephen Tolbert, the brother of the Vice-President, who was then the Secretary of Commerce. I was not startled when, in my interview with him, he stated that the government was considering subsidizing Japanese fisherman to establish an industry based in Monrovia instead of encouraging Liberian fishermen to expand their operations. Even more recently, when asked about the large number of Lebanese in the country, Tubman responded that Liberians had no business acumen and should learn how to trade from the Lebanese.[8]

The situation in the commerical and light-industrial sectors of the economy also applies to agricultural production: the major effort is under the direct control of Firestone, Goodrich, and other foreign concessionaires. Of the eleven leading independent producers, all but two of the farms were owned by families of previous Presidents of Liberia or by individuals who had served in the Tubman administration at one stage or another. Prominent in the top twenty-five producers were members of the cabinet,

[8] *West Africa,* 25 April 1964.

leading legislators, and even district commissioners. The last-named frequently owned farms in the districts where they were serving despite the explicit ban in the Liberian Code of Laws on conflict of interest in the Department of Internal Affairs.

THE ALIEN SAFETY VALVE

How then does one account for the economic survival of Liberia and its current economic boom? Aside from the tribal people, who have in the past been employed on various projects on a compulsory labor basis and who still are employed largely at marginal wages, the economy of the Americo-Liberians has been supported by external sources. American and other missionary societies have from the outset provided funds, equipment, and personnel for the bulk of the education and health services in Liberia. It was not until the Tubman administration that any considerable portion of the government's budget was allocated to these ends. Similarly, the capital and managerial skill required to exploit Liberia's agricultural and mineral resources has been secured from foreign sources, with Firestone Plantations and the various mining and other concessions owned and operated by Americans, Germans, Scandinavians, Swiss, and other non-Liberians. The merchandising of commodities is largely in the hands of Lebanese and Syrians. Even the large rubber and fruit plantations owned by the Americo-Liberian elite are in many cases managed by West Indians, Sierra Leoneans, and other non-Liberian Negroes. It must be noted, too, that the various foreign aid programs of the American and other friendly governments have been providing capital, technical skill, and education on an increasing scale since the end of the Second World War. The consequences of this were noted by the economic survey team of Northwestern University, which suggested that

It is only a slight exaggeration to say that the professional, managerial, and entrepreneurial labor force in Liberia is divided neatly into two groups: Liberians work for government, are owners of rubber farms, transport facilities, and buildings, provide legal services, and to a small extent medical and commercial services. Foreigners are overwhelmingly predominant in staff positions in iron ore, rubber, and timber. Where Liberians are employed by concessions, they most frequently act as nonresident advisers in law, public relations and advertising.[9]

This heavy reliance upon alien personnel led the Northwestern group to refer to the economic experiment in Liberia during the Tubman era as a case of "growth without development." This situation will be analyzed further in Chapter 9.

Obviously, the alien supporters of Liberia feel that there are worthwhile goals to be achieved by continuing to buttress the economy. Each venture, however, brings an exaction for the Americo-Liberian group. Even the missionary whose goal is the winning of converts to Christianity is required by law to establish a school before he can pursue his calling. Each new concession agreement or renewal of an old agreement brings increased benefits for the Whig-controlled government or new positions and enterprises that will accrue to the Whig leadership. The advantage for the Whig Party in dealing with alien entrepreneurs rather than middle-class Liberians is that the former are in the

[9] Robert W. Clower, George Dalton, Mitchell Harwitz, and A. A. Walters, *op. cit.*, p. 275.

country on sufferance. As aliens (and in the case of non-Negroes, this means permanent aliens, for they are ineligible for citizenship), the twenty thousand Americans, Lebanese, Europeans, and Israelis cannot own real estate, engage in certain reserved occupations, or become involved in the political process as members of a political party or pressure group. The depoliticization of the most significant groups in the Liberian economy thus serves as a safety valve for the Whigs against a tribal-based revolution achieving its goal via the economic route.

Religious Structures

As with economic groupings, the potentially independent role of religious associations in the Liberian political process is narrowly circumscribed. A loose form of interlocking directorates ensures that the clergy of most Protestant churches, the lay organization within the Episcopal and Roman Catholic churches, and the officers of the YMCA and other semireligious societies remain under Whig Party control. It is possible for a small community preacher to use his pulpit as a springboard for political advancement, but in most instances the process is reversed. Almost by right, prominent political figures can claim high office in a religious organization. Thus, Vice-President William Tolbert, who in 1966 served as international president of the Baptist World Alliance, was earlier elected president of the Liberian Baptist Missionary and Educational Convention, beating out a candidate who was only a member of the House of Representatives. Another member of the Legislature, Rep. J. J. Mends-Cole, is head moderator of the Presbyterian Church. In fact, many of the Protestant ministers must, to maintain a decent standard of living, divide their time between their congregation and a government job. Hence, their reforming zeal in both the religious and political realms is necessarily blunted. In addition to churches, it is worth noting that the last fourteen Worshipful Grand Masters of the Masons include three Presidents, one Vice-President, a Speaker of the House, Chief Justice and Associate Justice of the Supreme Court, an Attorney General, and other leading officials.

Religious office undoubtedly reinforces the political standing of an individual, for the style of Liberian politics demands that officials attend church and even preach sermons or read the lesson. The speeches of President Tubman, who is himself a Methodist preacher, are laced with Biblical references. When, for example, he was asked in May, 1962, about his intentions regarding a fifth term, he sent reporters to their Bibles to discover the message of Isaiah: 49 ("Thus saith the Lord: In an acceptable time I have heard thee, and in the day of salvation I have helped thee. I have preserved thee and given thee to be a Covenant of the people."). Certain churches, such as the First Methodist Church and Trinity Episcopal Cathedral, are regarded as "political" in the sense that some of the leading figures in the "honorable" class are members. A younger political leader, attempting to establish an independent base for movement upward in the political scale, may attempt to become the person of influence in one of the smaller churches in Monrovia. The correlation between religious and political office was certainly made evident during one meeting the author attended of the vestry of a Monrovia church. In a blatant fashion a man who only a few days previously had been removed from office by the

President found himself stripped by the vestry of his post as senior warden in the church.

No particular effort is made by the Americo-Liberian elite to control the Bassa Community Church and other nativistic religious groups, although there was great concern in the 1920's about the spread of Islam into Liberia. It is apparent, however, that the Mandingo and other Muslims have not attempted in recent years to secure political objectives at variance with the objectives of the Americo-Liberian community. It is significant that the "Muslim" leader who presented a petition to Tubman in 1960 to run for a fifth term was Momolu Dukuly. Five years previously, when Dukuly was the Liberian Secretary of State, he traveled abroad to represent his country at the Methodist General Conference.

Despite the official posture, repeated in 1967 by President Tubman himself, that Liberia observes a strict separation of church and state, this is not the case. The Jehovah's Witnesses, for example, have been arrested and harassed for failing to salute the flag. Far from being neutral, indeed, the political leadership of Liberia regards the churches as instrumental to the continuation of the existing power relation. In turn, a good political leader is expected to "raise the offering" in support of church activities. President Tubman's effort in this regard during one session of the Maryland County National Executive Council illustrates both his effectiveness and "impartiality." It was reported that

. . . in his hometown he sponsored a rally for Mount Scott Methodist Church of which he is a member and raised $15,000 in less than an hour. At the Mount Tubman Methodist Church built in 1899 under the pastorage of the late

Reverend Alexander Tubman, his father, he assisted in raising $2,531.91. At St. Mark's Protestant Episcopal Church he raised $500. Whilst in Grand Cess he and his suite contributed $800 toward the Christian and educational efforts in that area. Of this amount the Catholic Church received $300 and the Robertson Memorial Methodist Church got the balance of $500.[10]

Finally, it might be noted, the Masonic Order, with W. V. S. Tubman as chairman of its Building Committee, never really doubted that its splendid new temple in Monrovia would be completed.

Social and Charitable Organizations

Next to involvement in politics, membership in social organizations is the most dominant characteristic of Americo-Liberian life. Indeed, membership in such organizations, as is true of religious participation, advances and reinforces a political career. Conviviality and "running with a crowd" are marks of a successful politician, one who shares his good fortune with his fellows, who gossips and publicly speculates instead of being introverted and secretive about his affairs, and who capitalizes upon the friendships and knowledge he has gained through social interaction in securing his own position and thus preserving the kind of society in which the Americo-Liberians can continue to dominate. Most of the social clubs are small, a dozen or two members at most, and bring together a cluster of individuals of approximately the same age and from the same community. Many of these ties were formed in school. To a certain degree the members of a group rise

[10] Department of State, Bureau of Information, "National Unification" (May, 1954), p. 11.

together in the political system. Among the more important are several with such quaint names as the Crowd 15, the Hungry Club, the Saturday Afternoon Club, the Triple Six, the Crowd Three Times, Crowd 12, Crowd 13, "Coba," and the Moonlight Sonata Club.

Involvement in charitable organizations serves other functions. Participation as a sponsor of the Boy Scouts, the Girl Guides, the Red Cross, and other groups provides a political leader with a base from which he may demonstrate publicly his concern for the poor. One political leader in the Boy Scout movement (which was not officially recognized by the international organization at that time) was quite cynical about the benefits the office brought him. "People *do* contribute to the Scouts, you know," he said. "And I have gone abroad twice to present our case to the international headquarters." Hikes, campouts, and the usual activities of Boy Scouts, however, were nowhere apparent. A leading officer of the Red Cross, moreover, made a considerable personal profit from the sale of potatoes donated for relief purposes by an American naval vessel on a good-will visit.

Thrift, credit, and social clubs similar to the Monrovia "crowds" have been formed among the tribal people who have migrated to the urbanized centers. Even a Liberian War Veterans Association—largely tribal in membership —flourishes in Monrovia. Such groups are permitted and even encouraged, provided that the leadership abstains from using the organization as a political pressure group. The Americo-Liberian rulers are far less permissive with respect to various associations involving the tribal inhabitants of the interior. The creation of social clubs involving only educated tribal youths in many areas constitutes prima-facie evidence of subversion. An absolute ban still prevails with respect to traditional groups, such as the Leopard Society, which are organized to commit murder, cannibalism, and other crimes. Equally proscribed is the Mende tribe's Baboon Society, which in the immediate pre-Tubman era was implicated in an alleged plot to destroy the Americo-Liberian aristocracy.[11]

The most prominent and prevalent of tribal traditional organizations—the men's Poro and the women's Sande societies—have, however, been permitted to function now that they have been brought under government control. The historic fears of the Americo-Liberians regarding the power of the Poro were probably not exaggerated. It was the Poro societies, after all, which fomented the uprisings of 1898 in neighboring Sierra Leone against the extension of British and Creole influence into the tribal hinterland of that country. The alliance launched in the last century between the Whigs and the traditional chiefs, the political and administrative fragmentation of some of the larger tribal groupings, and other measures have been employed in emasculating the political powers of the Poro leadership. The licensing of *zoes* and other Poro officials and the naming of President Tubman as the head of all Poros has not only given the President an added popular base, but it also gives the executive a measure of supervisory control. As educational, health, and other facilities of the national government are extended to the interior, the functions of the Poro will be more and more reduced. Ultimately, it may come to have the same curiosity and propaganda value

[11] Accounts of the trial of prominent persons who were implicated in the plot against Barclay are contained in the 1940 issues of the *African Nationalist* (Library of Congress microfilm).

for the Unification Policy as the Vai script, which the Liberian government is now taking great pains to publicize as an example of indigenous African writing.[12] Since the Poro has been brought under a degree of political control, and, moreover, its bush schools, medicine, and community dancing keep the tribal people contented, the government feels it can view the institution with indulgence.

Students and the Educational System

In the long run, students may provide one of the key elements in accelerating the pace of genuine social reform in Liberia. This would be a decided reversal of function for the Liberian educational system, which, prior to the Tubman regime, constituted one of the significant reinforcing mechanisms for the maintenance of the castelike relationship that developed in Liberia during the nineteenth century. During most of Liberia's history education remained the monopoly of the elite. Although staffed and financed largely by American and other foreign missionaries, control over the school system remained largely in the hands of the upper strata of America-Liberian society resident at the coast. Missionaries, in obtaining the privilege of recruiting new members, have been required by law to provide school facilities. Political intervention by the Americo-Liberian "honorables" was so strong that the missions were obliged to concentrate upon the children from settler families even when the schools were located a few miles out of Monrovia or the other coastal towns. It was only in the period following the Second World War, when missionaries were permitted to stake out new terri-

[12] Gail Stewart, "Notes on the Present-day Usage of the Vai Script in Liberia," *African Language Review,* VI (1967), 71–74.

tories in the remote interior, that the tribal child was given even a fair chance of a modern education. In some areas, such as the Kpelle districts in Bong County, the Lutherans, Methodists, and Episcopalians are now actually training the second generation of modernized Kpelle youth. This has had a significant impact upon both the quantity and the quality of tribal participation in the administration of the county.

There are dangers in overstressing the revolutionary role played by foreign technicians, as was done by Fletcher Knebel in his novel *The Zinzin Road,* or has been done by the Liberian government in its dismissal of two Peace Corps teachers in 1968. Nevertheless, the American Peace Corps group and AID have constituted forces for change. It was probably only the prodding of AID with regard to the construction of new schools in the interior that has partially corrected the gross educational imbalance between the coast and the hinterland. The Peace Corps volunteer, moreover, has provided one of the few examples to tribal children of a dedicated and impartial teacher who has had no vested political or religious interest to pursue. The volunteer has been a full-time instructor rather than one who has had to "moonlight" (often at the direct financial expense of his students) in order to secure a living wage. The Peace Corpsman's use of standardized English better prepares the student for his advanced studies than the Liberian form of English—or even pidgin English—to which tribal students were often exposed in the past. Significantly, the impact of the Peace Corps presence is frequently as strong upon the Liberian teachers as it is upon the students.

Although professionalism has provided a degree of

"class" interest on the part of primary and secondary school teachers, political control over the school system remains fairly secure at this point. The appointment of teachers constitutes a political act, and assignment to a particular institution is based upon the influence and political loyalty of the teacher's family. As with all other governmental employees, teachers are required to surrender a month's salary each year to the support of the True Whig Party. The eagerness with which school superintendents and principals leave their posts to run for office or accept a nonacademic post in government is some measure of the low level of professionalism even at the upper reaches of school administration.

The conservative character of the higher educational system has also been long apparent. The University of Liberia, founded as Liberia College in 1862, was almost entirely limited to the Americo-Liberian group prior to 1950. The curriculum was weighted overwhelmingly in favor of politics and the law, and prior to Tubman, no attention was given to practical matters such as agriculture, engineering, forestry, veterinary science, or commerce. Even during the period of my research, university lecturers for the most part held elective or appointive offices in government, and the board of trustees included five Senators, five Representatives, and seven appointees of the President. Neither the faculty nor the board could be expected to challenge the fundamental structure of Liberian society. The students as well have been members of the Establishment, and the graduation roster of the University of Liberia has read like a "Who Will Be Who" of future governments of Liberia. Friendship ties forged during their college days have been directly responsible for the political success of members of a given graduating class, and this has been a factor in maintaining Americo-Liberian elite solidarity. The four graduates of the Class of 1944, for example, had by 1968 come to play a critical role in Liberian politics, holding the posts of Secretary of State, Director-General of National Public Health Services, president of the University of Liberia, and ambassador to an important African state. Indeed, 80 per cent of the surviving members of the graduating classes of 1934 through 1949 held significant posts in the cabinet, the Legislature, the more important ambassadorial positions, and the senior ranks of the bureaucracy in 1968. Regardless of subsequent educational experience abroad, attendance at the University of Liberia has been one of the evident criteria for political success in the Republic.

As long as the educational system remained small, it was possible to control its output in terms of preserving the *status quo*. The expansion of the primary and secondary school network into the interior has called for a complementary expansion of the pool of teachers. This has meant recruitment from one of three sources, each a potential threat to the regime: the tribal element; expatriates, who might be committed to idealism, materialism, or some other philosophy disruptive of Whig supremacy; or the poorer and less influential members of the Americo-Liberian community. The last group might constitute the greatest threat. Resentful of being deprived of his "heritage" and regarding a post in the interior as a form of exile far removed from the political and social rewards of Monrovia, the lower-class Americo-Liberian frequently exploits the tribal people more than the members of the ruling aristocracy. Less interested in preserving a system that has denied him his "just due," he tends to be less restrained in his arrogance toward the tribal people.

The current generation of students, moreover, gravely concerns the ruling elite. The expansion of the foreign scholarship programs of the American, West German, Israeli, and other governments has broadened the opportunity for tribal-educated youths. The sheer magnitude of the scholarship programs makes it difficult to limit the opportunities merely to deserving members of the upper strata of Liberian society. Increasingly, too, the terms of a grant emphasize training in engineering, agriculture, and other fields that could contribute to the development of a pool of nonpolitical technocrats opposed to the inefficiencies of the present political system. With this potential threat in mind, the Liberian government in September, 1962—when generous fellowship offers were coming in from all quarters of the globe—insisted (as many African governments now do) that all foreign fellowships were to be channeled through, and awarded by, the Liberian government.

Like those who go abroad, however, students who receive their secondary or higher education within Liberia may constitute an equally disturbing element. In fact, by creaming off the Americo-Liberian progeny for study abroad, the foreign fellowship program has increased the prospects of tribal youth and poorer Americo-Liberians securing admission to the University of Liberia and the mission-run colleges. In the late 1950's strikes at Cuttington College and at the Seventh Day Adventist Academy at Konala provided some index of student restiveness. By 1963, Tubman had become so alarmed by the strident demands of students that he attempted to link the faculty and students at Cuttington, the College of West Africa (a Methodist high school), and even the University of Liberia with an alleged military plot against his government. He labeled these institutions breeding grounds for "socialistic and subversive ideas" and put the leadership on notice that the institutions would be closed down if passions were not controlled. Tubman stated that he could not object to the socialist tendencies of his African neighbors (presumably Nkrumah and Touré), but that Liberians would "fight to the death any attempt to impose or force upon us what we consider a mystical illusion." [13]

The Role of The Military

An even more serious threat to Americo-Liberian supremacy than the protest of students and teachers is the developing professionalization of the police and the military. Elsewhere in Africa the spectre of military power has challenged, and in several instances has dislodged, political party leadership. The size of the military component, moreover, seems not to be a factor. Indeed, nowhere in Africa during the colonial period was the army larger than necessary for the maintenance of public order, and the forces were shifted about to suit the occasion. Nor has the military's lack of training in the art of governing prevented it from wresting control from the politicians. Military "government" exists only in the sense that the generals or colonels have the active support of bureaucrats, educators, technicians, and even the "reformed" politicians. The military provides either a balance wheel or a veto group in this coalition of forces that has carried on after the dominant party leadership has been deposed.

[13] *Listener Daily,* 16 Feb. 1963, pp. 1, 10.

Recognizing the potential threat, party leaders in East and West Africa have employed various techniques to keep the military on tap rather than on top. In Guinea, for example, Sékou Touré put his army to work in community development schemes when he was faced with the mass return of pensionless veterans following the rupture with de Gaulle in 1958. Nyerere, following the army mutiny of 1964, created a citizens' army which has become an extension of the Tanzanian African National Union and a positive instrument in carrying out his policies of "self-reliance." In Uganda the present leaders have attempted to rely on the less-modernized Nilotic peoples of the north as the significant element in the armed forces, hoping thereby to stay the political ambitions of the more advanced Baganda and other Bantu groups.

Prior to 1908 the Americo-Liberians relied upon either foreign assistance or hastily organized "home guard" units to defend the settler communities against tribal attacks. The units normally consisted of an Americo-Liberian officer in the militia who recruited his troops from among the poorer class of Americo-Liberians, tribal wards, and friendly tribal persons whose "loyalty" to the Americo-Liberians had been demonstrated. Once the threatening situation had abated, the organization largely dissolved. In 1908, however, the menacing posture of both France and Britain along Liberia's frontiers convinced the Liberian government that it should regularize its system of control over the people in the border areas, and the Liberian Frontier Force was established to carry out police, customs, and other functions in the hinterland.

As long as the Liberian Frontier Force remained small and its mission was limited to the control of poorly organized and poorly armed tribal rebels, it was a structure of support for the Whig aristocracy. The officer class—drawn almost exclusively from the Americo-Liberian group or from tribal elites with firm links to the ruling group—was selected largely on the basis of patronage. The general lack of professional training did not give the officers any motivation to alter an inefficient political system in the way that the technologically concerned officer groups have done in many Asian and Middle Eastern states. Equally satisfied with the *status quo* were the tribal people recruited to serve in the ranks. The low salary was more than compensated for by the prestige of the uniform and the carte blanche that members of the Force had in exploiting the communities in which they have been stationed. It was a matter of policy not to post an enlisted man to his home area, and thereby the army avoided possible conflicts of loyalty.

Events of the past decade, however, have made new demands upon the Force, which was restyled the National Guard in 1962. The presence of a large number of aliens throughout the hinterland in connection with the expanding economic and educational enterprises as well as the problems of illicit diamond and gold mining operations have increased the training needs with respect to internal security. (Ordinary police functions have now been assumed by the Liberian National Police Force.) External threats, real or imagined, have intensified concern, too, for the more rapid professionalization of the armed forces: several times during recent years rumors have run through Monrovia that Guinean forces had marched across the border and claimed Nimba Mountain. Finally, Liberia's new role in intra-African politics has affected its military preparedness. Liberia's debut in that role during the Congo crisis showed in a rather embarrassing way the inadequacy of the Liberian troops' training. Since that experience the Liberian government has been more receptive to the suggestions for training made by the United States military mission. Gradually the military structure has been reorganized along more professional lines and modernized in many respects.

Professionalism, however, threatens old political practices. The military leaders, as well as the American donors, are becoming increasingly annoyed with the illegal use of soldiers and military equipment for the cultivation of crops and road construction on the farms of "honorables." The military spectre itself was raised in February, 1963, when the head of the National Guard, Colonel David Thompson, and others were arrested to forestall an alleged coup. Colonel Thompson was reported to have said that "if only 250 Togolese soldiers could kill President Olympio and overthrow his government, an army of 5,000 in Liberia can do wonders." [14] Again, during the unrest following the labor strikes of 1966, Tubman dramatically announced that a foreign power (never named) had attempted to bribe army officers to stage a coup during the President's pending health leave in Switzerland.

Despite the challenge of the military, the responses of the Americo-Liberians to labor disturbances and disorders involving the tribal inhabitants has been to increase rather than decrease the role of the military. The emergency powers given the President during the Firestone strike of February, 1966, authorized him to increase the size of the army by five thousand men, call into service young recruits

[14] *Ibid.,* 6 Feb. 1963, p. 1; and subsequent issues.

on an emergency basis, and even to mobilize civilians. Indeed, under Colonel George T. Washington, who was appointed Army Chief of Staff in 1965, the army has been expanded and steps have been taken to establish the National Military Academy that the Legislature gave Tubman as a "birthday present" on his seventieth birthday. No attempt, however, has been made to capture the political commitment of the professionalized officer class. On the other hand, little has been done to reorganize the citizen militia, estimated at twenty thousand; but this may be a source of support for the Americo-Liberians in any future contest between the government and a professionalized army. The militia (which is similar to the politically controlled National Guard in many of the American states) carries out its training program in a most lax and casual fashion. It is drawn largely from the ranks of the Americo-Liberian class and tribal persons who have long years of residence in the more urbanized areas at the coast.

CHAPTER 6

The True Whig Party

Another defense of Americo-Liberian privilege has been the perpetuation of the single-party system.[1] During the many years of challenge from the tribal people and the European colonial powers in the neighboring dependencies, the solidarity of the Americo-Liberian community was maintained by the political monopoly the True Whig Party has enjoyed since the election of 1877. The Unification Policy and the various political reforms introduced under the Tubman regime have made the single-party system even more indispensable to the maintenance of Whig supremacy. Patronage continues to be the primary weapon used to keep the party faithful in line and to undermine the opposition by seduction of its qualified leadership. The True Whig Party nevertheless has had to adjust to the times and innovate, if only to give the appearance of democratic reform.

This compels the leadership of the True Whig Party to provide more than perfunctory observance of the cardinal democratic procedural norm: elections. The elaborate and extended ritual of petitioning the President and other candidates to seek re-election, the lively nominating conventions, the campaigning that carries candidates into the

[1] Sections of this chapter have appeared previously in my chapter on Liberia in Coleman and Rosberg, eds., *op. cit.* I am indebted to the University of California Press for their permission to republish sections of that study here.

smallest backwater communities, the colorful and often humorous political posters, and the element of suspense regarding the counting of votes on election day might convince the casual observer that the results of the election were actually in doubt and that the opposition party had an outside chance of unseating the Whig candidates.

Little, however, is left to chance. The Party fears that the license permitted the opposition during an election might encourage them to regard a substantial electoral showing as a precursor of better things to come; exploiting the cleavages within the ranks of the Americo-Liberians, they might even resort to violence to achieve their objectives. The assassination attempt against Tubman in 1955 reveals that violence has actually been resorted to on occasion when the opposition feels that the channels for orderly change of government personnel are closed.[2]

The control over the electoral system begins with the naming of the Elections Commission. In theory the Commission is nonpartisan and the façade is maintained by the requirement that members must, when appointed, renounce all party affiliations. True Whig dominance, however, is assured by the proviso that the President names not only the chairman and the Whig Party representative to the commission but also selects the third member from a list of candidates submitted by the opposition parties. One of the key duties of the Commission is the determination of whether a candidate or a party is entitled to a place on the official ballot. In 1951, for example, the Reformation Party was declared an illegal group by the Commission

[2] For an official version of the attempt, see Liberian Information Service, *The Plot That Failed* (London: Consolidated Publications, 1959).

and denied the right to contest Tubman's bid for a second term. The Reformation Party had been formed by dissident Kru under the leadership of Didhwo Twe, once considered a close friend of the President's. In 1955 the Legislature made the decision easier for the Commission, outlawing by statute both the Independent True Whig Party and the Reformation Party "because of their dangerous, unpatriotic, unconstitutional, illegal, and conscienceless acts. . . ." [3] Both parties supported former President Edwin Barclay, who was challenging his hand-picked successor.

Restrictions on Public Dissent

Even if the opposition group is permitted a place on the ballot, the Whig Party's near-monopoly over the principal channels of communication has the opposition at a decided disadvantage. The government-owned *Liberian Age* and *Liberian Star* as well as the privately owned but government-subsidized *Daily Listener* have, in the past, observed almost a conspiracy of silence with respect to opposition parties that threaten to be even moderately successful in their appeal. Journalists who work for the government press, moreover, find themselves on occasion being held "in contempt of the Legislature" or in other ways punished for any unsanctioned criticism of the government policy or a member of the "honorable" class. Indeed, in 1966 the editor of the government-owned *Liberian Star* was imprisoned for "improprieties." Imprisonment is a frequent fate of opposition editors who find themselves running afoul of the highly restrictive and capriciously enforced libel law, which gives the President and other leading officials of government immunity

[3] *Liberian Code,* title 12, ch. 8, sec. 216.

from ordinary criticism. Recent Liberian political history has been checkered by the suppression of private newspapers such as *The Friend* (1954) and the *Independent* (1955) and the arrest of their staffs. The editor of the *African Nationalist* lingered fifteen years in prison before his release in 1966. One inveterate and irrepressible pamphleteer in Montserrado County, because of age, family esteem, and the political utility of some of his criticism, thus far has been able to escape with little more than a brief jail sentence, dismissal from his job, or public rebuke by the press or the Legislature. There are other pieces of evidence, too, which suggest that a certain amount of "loyal" criticism is permitted in the editorials, letters to the editor, and even straight news stories, providing that the political leader criticized is not of very high rank or the policy too vital to the stability of the regime. Indeed, it has been strongly suggested that press criticism is a circuitous means whereby the President puts a miscreant official "on notice."

In addition to governmental censorship, the opposition party and its leadership may find itself subjected to various forms of harassment. Didhwo Twe, the Kru leader who challenged Tubman in the election of 1951, was obliged to flee the country on the eve of the election. In his final election speech, Tubman charged that Twe's hands were "stained with the blood of treason, rebellion and sedition. He has been unfaithful and recreant to his trust as a Liberian citizen." [4] His major sin, apparently, was to emphasize too strongly his Kru antecedents. Tubman's next opponent, ex-President Edwin Barclay, found the efforts of

[4] Reginald Townsend, ed., *President Tubman of Liberia Speaks* (London: Consolidated Publications, 1959), p. 99. Twe fled from Liberia in 1951 during the electoral campaign. He remained in

his coalition Independent True Whig and Reformation parties in 1955 equated with treason to the Liberian state. He even found his campaign impeded by an official investigation, with a vague charge of attempted murder being leveled against him.

Finally, throughout every campaign the activities of the opposition partisans are reported to the President by his "liaison and relations officers," who are stationed in every county and territory in the republic. The duty of these officers, according to the Liberian Code, is to provide for "the prevention of subversive activity and dissemination of dangerous propaganda." [5] The Secretary of the Treasury has a statutory mandate to provide for their salaries.

Public criticism of the True Whig Party is regarded as a threat to the solidarity of the Americo-Liberian community, exposing it to challenges from the tribal majority. Public disagreement raises the spectre of a dissident settler group tipping the political scales in its own favor by forming an alliance that crosses the cultural line dividing the Whigs and the tribal element. Public dissension also tarnishes the image of the "New Liberia" which the leadership is attempting to project in its intra-African relations. [6]

---

exile in Sierra Leone until 1960, when Tubman granted him "pardon and freedom from prosecution" (*Liberian Age,* 17 June 1960, p. 1).

[5] *Liberian Code,* title 13, sec. 12.

[6] It is especially offensive when criticisms of Liberia are made abroad. Former Attorney-General C. A. Cassell found himself disbarred for life for having criticized the Liberian judiciary at the Lagos Conference of Jurists in 1961. His remarks, oddly enough, were less offensive than the indictment against the same judiciary by A. Dash Wilson upon assuming the office of Chief Justice a few years previously. *Liberian Age,* 3 March 1961, p. 4.

The Function of Elections

If the opposition party perseveres till election day, there is still no assurance that its partisans will be permitted to vote or that their votes will even be counted. In the 1955 election the ballots cast for the Independent True Whig Party were counted in only two counties. If the ballots are counted and a majority is recorded, there is no assurance that the victory will be recognized. After the 1931 election in Maryland County the Legislature in a naked display of power simply refused to seat the candidates of the People's Party who had defeated the True Whigs by 1676 votes to 367.[7]

Nonetheless, Liberian elections are not entirely meaningless. There is, first of all, the observance of constitutional norms, which apparently have a high value to the legally minded Americo-Liberians. Secondly, it does provide for at least a biennial discussion of the party's goals and permits new generations to be socialized to the purposes and leadership of the party. Not only policies but the personnel of government change as a result of this active discussion. Following each election the President considers that he has a new mandate and may shuffle executive appointments without having to justify dismissals and additions as he would in midterm.

The most significant function of elections in Liberia, however, is the maintenance of a good image abroad. Despite Whig trepidations about elections and despite the measures taken to emasculate the opposition, Whig leaders publicly insist that opposition is healthy for the Republic. On the eve of both the 1955 and the 1959 elections, for ex-

[7] *African Nationalist,* 8 Nov. 1941, p. 3.

ample, President Tubman indicated that he was going to vote for his opponent, "even though it may not be in accordance with the law. . . ." [8] His opponent, Circuit Court Judge William O. Davies-Bright, was a True Whig running as an Independent on the policy of "sincerity, purity, and peace." He stated after the election of 1955 that had he known of Mr. Tubman's voting for him, he would have voted for Tubman. With only 16 votes for Davies-Bright and 244,937 votes for Tubman, the former had very few to spare. In the election of 1959, Davies-Bright got 55 votes to Tubman's 530,566. As the Judge stated, he only ran in response to Tubman's call for "fair and friendly competition." Not inappropriately, the party symbol on the ballot for Davies-Bright was a sheep. Largely in response to a suggestion from President John F. Kennedy, Tubman permitted token opposition—at least during the campaign stage—in his fifth bid for the presidency in 1963. By 1967 he no longer felt it was necessary to continue the charade or else he felt that an opposition campaign could be a threat to stability in view of the wave of strikes in 1966.

Despite its almost complete annihilation of opposition party movements, the Whig leadership abhores violence and extended controversy. Indeed, the rancor following the election of 1955, which led ultimately to an assassination attempt against President Tubman as well as the subsequent indiscriminate prosecution of members of the opposition, is rare for Liberian politics.[9] Typically, the "hand of forgiveness" is extended to dissident Whigs who

[8] *Liberian Age,* 6 May 1959, p. 1; *Daily Listener,* 21 Feb. 1959, p. 1 and 24 Feb. 1959, p. 1.

[9] Liberian Information Service, *The Plot That Failed.*

lead opposition movements. This is an old pattern in Liberian politics. In Liberia's first election as a republic, Joseph Jenkins Roberts named his defeated opponent as the first Chief Justice of the Liberian Supreme Court. In 1912, following a bitterly contested election of the preceding year, President Daniel Howard named his opponent president of Liberia College and subsequently Chief Justice. Again, during Tubman's first administration he went so far as to establish a coalition cabinet by naming leaders of the Unit Whig Party and the People's Party to executive posts including the very important position of Secretary of the Department of the Interior (now Internal Affairs). The experiment was short-lived, however, for it had the undesired effect of giving second parties public status and access to patronage.[10]

Internal Party Organization

The True Whig Party is the only political organization in Liberia that functions on a continuing basis. Opposition parties are highly personalized affairs organized to compete in specific elections and rally under the banner of a dissident Whig. In at least four instances in this century, the opposition leader has been a former President. The hastily contrived campaign staff is disbanded once the party has met its inevitable defeat, and a new band of dissidents takes up the opposition in a subsequent election. Although there was a measure of continuity in leadership between the People's Party of 1923 and 1927, the repeated use of popular opposition labels gives a false impression of

[10] In 1966, Tubman personally went to the prison cell and pardoned one of the individuals convicted in the 1955 assassination attempt.

continuity between, for example, the Republican Party of 1883 and 1911, the People's Party of 1927 and 1943, the Unit Whig Party of 1935 and 1943, or the Reformation Party of 1951 and 1955. The informality of opposition party procedures is illustrated by the "convention" of the Independent True Whig Party, which was formed in 1955. A hundred or more dissident Whigs met in the home of ex-President Edwin Barclay to nominate him for the presidency. So pressed was Barclay for fellow partisans that the convention nominated candidates for the Legislature without receiving their approval.

Opposition politics is normally an affair of the more politically alert counties: Montserrado and, occasionally, Maryland. In the remaining areas dissent is subject to greater restrictions by the ruling families, who are very much aware of their minority position vis-à-vis the tribal people. Normally, too, the opposition party concentrates upon the main political prize, the presidency. For this reason the opposition parties seldom make an appearance in the biennial elections for the Legislature.

In contrast to the ephemeral organization of the renegade Whigs, the apparatus of the True Whig Party has survived more than forty elections since its founding in 1869. There are various principles of organization evident in the party effort. Since the Tubman regime, for example, various specialized wings, based upon age or sex, have been formed to give additional foci to party activities. The primary principle of organization however is geographic. With the extension of legislative representation and almost universal suffrage to the people of the hinterland, this means that potentially every voting precinct within the Republic can be organized into a local chapter of the

True Whig Party. The local chapters are loosely affiliated into what are, in effect, two separate Whig Parties. The first is the National Whig Party, which meets every eight or four years to nominate presidential and vice-presidential candidates. The second is the county or territorial Whig Party, which meets at least every two years in convention to nominate candidates for the Legislature. The autonomy of each convention was revealed in 1959 at the county conventions, which met after the national convention had renominated President Tubman. Proposed resolutions endorsing the nominations made by the national conclave were objected to by various delegates as an attempt on the part of the county party to "review the decisions of the National party." [11]

THE NATIONAL CONVENTION

The national convention meets every eight or four years, depending upon whether the President is in his first or a subsequent term. Normally, the meeting is held in Monrovia during January, more than three months in advance of the May elections and more than eleven months prior to the beginning of a new administration. Only twice since 1912, however, has "lame-duck-ism" been a problem in Liberia. The principal task of the convention is the nomination of presidential and vice-presidential candidates. The "dumping" of a Vice-President by the President does give the convention a greater choice in the selection of this candidate than it has in the naming of a national standard-bearer. Only four times in the present century has an incumbent President decided to retire and permit the convention to name a candidate.

[11] *Daily Listener,* 27 Feb. 1959, *et seq.*

At least publicly, the conventions of 1919 and 1934 seemed to be lively affairs, with several contenders competing for the votes of the delegates. In 1943, Clarence Simpson, S. David Coleman, James F. Cooper, and Louis A. Grimes were actively considered, and various individuals were placed in nomination. Actually, the *African Nationalist,* a leading paper during the Barclay administration, provided a clue regarding Barclay's possible choice through its detailed reporting of every movement of Associate Justice William V. S. Tubman during 1940 and 1941. More than fifteen months before the convention of 1943, the editor picked Tubman as the leading aspirant and noted that Tubman "has the whole of Maryland County, and not a minor part of Montserrado, and everywhere his name is heard, it has a captivating charm, because he is a natural mixer of men, good manners, and some persons say —liqueurs." [12] Although the convention choice was apparently determined in advance, the intraparty struggle at the convention compelled Tubman to accept Simpson as his running mate and to name members from the opposition parties to his first administration. Thus, a latent function of the national convention at the time of a succession is to reveal the lines of factionalism within the party.

The ineffectiveness of the national convention as a constituent body that makes decisions independently of those arrived at by the party leadership is revealed by the flexible rules regarding membership in the convention. There is no allocation of a fixed number of seats to county and territorial units of the party. There is an informal understanding regarding those whose Whig credentials are in order and should be permitted to attend the conven-

[12] *African Nationalist,* 8 Nov. 1941, p. 1.

tion. The number of delegates may run from as low as three to four hundred, as in 1959, to several thousand, which was the case in 1955 when Tubman wanted to undercut the threat posed by the candidacy of former President Edwin Barclay.

The national convention performs other, less-publicized tasks. The party platform, for example, is formulated by leaders of the party and presented for approval. The relative unimportance of the platform is revealed in the failure of the leading papers to report its contents. Finally, the conventions elect the officers of the True Whig Party who will assist the President in the management of party affairs between conventions. The national chairman, the vice national chairman, the general secretary, the general treasurer, and the other elected members of the Executive Committee represent not only the trusted friends of the President but tend also to represent the Old Guard within the party.[13] The Executive Committee of the party also includes the President, leading members of the cabinet and the Legislature, and influential private citizens who the President feels should be included from time to time. The institution is loosely structured and its proceedings and significance vary according to the whim of the President, the *de facto* head of the True Whig Party.

[13] The Convention of 1959 elected Senator Edwin Morgan as National Chairman, Wilkin Tyler as Vice National Chairman, Postmaster-General McKinley DeShield as General Secretary, and former Secretary of the Treasury William Dennis as General Treasurer. DeShield became National Chairman upon the death of Morgan and has continued to hold that post.

Following an occasional American pattern, the national chairman of the True Whig Party has frequently been given the office of Postmaster General, although the predecessor of the present chairman was president pro tempore of the Senate. The continued confidence of Tubman in Chairman McKinley DeShield is revealed in the fact that he is the only cabinet officer who has survived the many shake-ups since Tubman took office in 1944. The national chairman of the party today, however, does not possess the same power in the field of patronage and other essential party matters that chairmen and general secretaries enjoyed prior to the presidency of Arthur Barclay (1904–1912). The resignation of President Coleman in 1900, for example, was in great measure forced by the public stand taken against Coleman's hinterland policies by T. W. Howard, who was national chairman of the party and Treasurer of the Republic, and by his son, Daniel E. Howard, who was at that time party secretary and governor of Montserrado County. Daniel Howard, in turn, was national chairman at the time of his election in 1911. His knowledge of patronage allocations and party decisions permitted him to consolidate his position as President quickly against the attempt of the strong-willed and very popular Barclay to exercise power behind the scenes following his retirement. It was Howard's experience, undoubtedly, which brought about the eclipse in the power of the national chairman and has left the office in the hands of those who have a strong allegiance to the President. Aside from his role in the investment and allocation of party funds and in the mediation of contests over candidacies for seats in the legislature, the chairman's duties relate largely to the organization of the national convention, the management of the presidential campaign, and the appointment of registrars and other election officials.

GEOGRAPHIC UNITS OF THE TRUE WHIG PARTY

The constituent body for the county and territorial units of the True Whig Party is the biennial convention that nominates candidates for the Legislature. In the case of the hinterland counties and territories, the selection of representatives is accomplished quickly. The county conventions at the coast, on the other hand, are much more active gatherings. This stems from the absence of clearly demarcated senatorial or representative districts, which compels the convention to adopt a single slate for the county at large to avoid opposition inroads at the polls. Certain principles have evolved to limit the intraparty struggle. In the case of senators, there was until the mid-1960's a fairly rigid rule that "each side of the river" within the county was to be represented. Secondly, there is an unwritten rule that each senator and representative is entitled to a second term, so that the issue of succession is foreclosed for eight or four years respectively. Although the tacit counterpart of this second rule is that no legislator is entitled to more than two terms, Speaker of the House Richard Henries and Representative J. J. Mends-Cole—to cite two exceptions—were elected in 1967 for their thirteenth and ninth terms. Tubman, moreover, made it explicit to a group from Montserrado County in 1962 that "there is no limit to the number of times a legislator may be re-elected to the House of Representatives." [14]

[14] *Liberian Age,* 3 Sept. 1962, p. 7.

One electoral issue that regularly generates intraparty conflict is representation in the House of Representatives for the various geographic areas within the coastal and hinterland countries. Letters to the editor of the *Liberian Age* reflect the general discontent over this problem which has implications of intertribal animosity in the interior and interfamily struggles for supremacy among the Whigs at the coast. As a consequence, it is not always possible for an outsider to predict the outcome of a county convention. In 1959, for example, at the Sinoe County preconvention caucus, Representative William Witherspoon turned back the challenge of H. C. Williamson, the Inspector of Mines, by 223 votes to 84. Although Witherspoon's name then was supposed to be the only one presented to the county convention to represent the precincts involved, the convention ended up nominating Williamson.[15] Although the appearance of decisional autonomy is thus maintained, contradictory evidence suggests that in this and other instances the national party leadership maintains a firm hand over the county convention proceedings and actually crushes attempts at rebellion on the part of the rank and file. There is, for example, the statement in the March 4, 1955, issue of the *Daily Listener,* owned and edited by Charles C. Dennis, nominee for the House of Representatives of the Montserrado County Convention. The Listener stated that the "result of the nomination was a bedrock conclusion that had been reached a day previous when shrewd politicians of the True Whig Party met at a caucus held at the Executive Mansion, the seat of the TWP standard bearer."[16] There was also the Grand Bassa

[15] *Daily Listener,* 27 Feb. 1959, p. 1, *Liberian Age,* 2 March 1959, p. 1.
[16] p. 1.

Convention of 1959, whose unanimous choice of a senatorial candidate was vetoed by the national party leadership. A second convention had to be held to renominate the incumbent Senator, who had irritated his constituents by his failure to visit Bassa between sessions. Tubman justified the reversal of the convention's original decision on the grounds that there had been a violation both of the two-term rule and of the stipulation that both sides of the St. John River were to be represented.[17]

There is no established pattern in the election of officers for the county organizations. The chairman may be the senior Senator or senior Representative or may hold an executive position, such as county superintendent. The chairman as well as the secretary and other key officers are usually acceptable to the leading families within the county. In the case of Montserrado County, which occupies such a pivotal role in Liberian politics, the confidence of the President is one of the key factors in selecting party officers for the county organization.

At the lowest level of party organization is the local branch, which may be limited to a single town or may embrace all of the towns and precincts included within the vaguely defined representative districts. The most obvious function of the local branches is to pass resolutions supporting presidential and legislative candidates. A new aspirant to office usually makes his case to the national leadership on the basis of the number of resolutions he has received from local branches of the party within his area. Certain local chapters of the party constitute very powerful units of the national and county party, and control over the organization is essential for the future of key poli-

17 *Liberian Age,* 27 Feb. 1959, p. 1; 2 March 1959, p. 1; 13 March 1959, p. 10; and *Daily Listener,* 3 March 1959, p. 1.

ticians. Speaker of the House Richard Henries, for example, has maintained his national influence through his chairmanship of the vital Monrovia local party, a position that he assumed in 1944.

SPECIALIZED UNITS OF THE PARTY

In the past few years the geographic units of the True Whig Party have been complemented by the establishment of specialized units to mobilize the energies of individuals who might not be adequately represented in the county or national parties. In 1958, for example, the Young People's Political Association of the Whig Party was formed in Maryland County and has since spread to the other counties. The youth association held its own convention shortly after the National Convention met in 1959 and has been active in legislative elections. There has been little likelihood that the association would become a focal point for opposition to the Old Guard. President Tubman's personal secretary, until his death in 1962 in an auto accident, was the first national chairman of the group.

A second specialized organization is the inevitable outgrowth of the granting of female suffrage during the Tubman administration. The Liberian Women Social and Political Movement was formed a few years ago by Sarah Simpson George, the sister of Tubman's first Vice-President and wife of one of the more influential representatives from Montserrado County. The present chairman of the movement is Doris Banks Henries, the wife of the Speaker of the House. Its primary goals are interesting the women of Liberia in politics and agitating for greater representation of women in the government of Liberia.

PARTY FINANCES

The method of financing the True Whig Party has remained substantially the same for several decades, although the details may change. Raymond Buell in 1928
reported that the Treasurer of Liberia automatically deducted 10 per cent of the monthly salary of every government employee until the expenses of the preceding
presidential campaign were met.[18] Doris Duncan Grimes,
the wife of the present Secretary of State and daughter of a
former cabinet officer, indicated even more recently that a
yearly "tax" was levied upon every public employee to the
extent of one month of his salary collected over a two-
month period.[19] There are other ways in which the party
coffers are replenished. Following his nomination, a candidate is expected to make generous contributions to the
national and county parties. The loser in a bitter party
struggle may also make a public offering to the party to
heal the breach and retain his membership in good standing. Finally, the Lebanese businessmen and other foreign
entrepreneurs are expected to contribute to the party in
the form of cash or by picking up the tab for party and official entertainment. Mrs. Grimes indicated that there had
never been a public accounting of the party funds. Various
sources have indicated that a European trading company
in Monrovia serves as the bank for the party.

In contrast to the True Whig Party, the patronage-poor
opposition party must be financed largely out of the per-

[18] *The Native Problem in Africa* (New York: Macmillan, 1928),
II, 712.
[19] "Economic Development on Liberia" (M.A. Thesis, New York
University, 1955), p. 6.

sonal fortunes of its leaders. Every effort is made by the Whig leadership to drain the opposition of its limited resources by constant litigation. In 1955, following Edwin Barclay's attempt to have the Legislature investigate the conduct of the election, the Legislature decided that Barclay should pay $19,000 as the estimated cost of the farcical and futile special session.

Conclusions

It is apparent that throughout much of Liberia's history the True Whig Party's monopolization of the electoral process has served as a strong bulwark of Americo-Liberian supremacy within the state. The techniques of controlling the machinery of organization, the procedures of nomination, and dissemination of information were learned well by the founders of the modern Liberian state. The façade of democracy and adherence to legalistic norms are maintained without surrendering to the possibility of open conflict within the ruling group—a situation that could only benefit the tribal majority.

CHAPTER 7

A "Family" Affair

Nominally, the Tubman reforms that introduced almost universal adult suffrage and have now extended the principle of direct legislative representation to the hinterland area have created an open political system. Even though electoral competition is effectively limited to a single party, membership in the True Whig Party is open to every adult citizen of the Republic without regard to cultural, ethnic, or religious origins. The only residents of the country excluded from politics are the twenty thousand aliens, many of whom have come to Liberia to engage in religious, educational, and economic activities. The majority of the aliens come from other African countries or the West Indies, and thus even they are eligible to vote once they have become naturalized citizens. The Constitution only denies citizenship to persons who lack Negro ancestry.[1]

On the face of it, the Liberian political system is highly democratic. The procedures whereby one becomes a member of the True Whig Party, and thus eligible for participation in national politics, are purposely vague. Although individuals are in some cases formally "read out" of the

[1] The Liberian Census of 1962 indicated that there were 21,365 aliens resident in the country. They came primarily from the following countries: Ghana (5,537), Guinea (4,110), Sierra Leone (2,084), Lebanon (2,077), U.S.A. (1,645), other African states (1,503), and West European states (3,233).

party by a local or national convention of the party due to the commission of certain "disloyal" acts, the more positive action of affiliation is apparently not signaled by any formal step on the part either of the member or the leadership. Any person can call himself a member on the basis of his participation in precinct or other local meetings of the party, by contributing funds to the organization or individual candidates, by marching in parades, by voting even in uncontested elections and by providing other outward signs of partisanship.

Circles of Involvement

Like participatory political systems anywhere, the Liberian political system can be viewed as a series of concentric circles, in which the outermost is least influential and the circles closer to the core have greater influence over the course of events and the actual decision-making process. Universal suffrage and the extension of the representative principle to all regions of Liberia have in theory made each participant in the outermost circle of political involvement equal in the election of a President and members of the Legislature. In fact, however, qualitative differences between residents of the coastal areas and those of the interior continue to exist despite the fact that under Tubman the tribal residents have been permitted to elect members to both the House of Representatives and the Senate. The extension of the county system in 1964, moreover, supposedly eliminated any administrative discrimination that might have resulted from the provincial system of rule in the hinterland.

Discrimination prior to 1964 stemmed from the fact that the four hinterland counties, which possessed 54 per cent of the population in 1962, were given eight senators as opposed to the ten controlled by the America-Liberian residents of the original five counties along the coast. The disparities in representation were even more apparent in the lower house of the Legislature. With 54 per cent of the population, the interior counties had only 20 per cent of the representation. Montserrado County was a special case of over-representation, with 23 per cent of the seats (nine of forty) with less than 16 per cent of the population. Moreover, Monsterrado County, as well as Tubman's own Maryland County, tended to monopolize the important committee assignments and chairmanships in the Legislature.

The second circle of political involvement is narrowed to those who participate in the nominating conventions for members of the Legislature. Although in theory a county convention is open to all who can make the journey to the county headquarters, the conventions are often limited to the elected and appointed officials of the Liberian government, former officials, prominent private citizens, and the camp followers of the leading committed candidates. Although the semblance of decisional autonomy is maintained, for the most part the nominations have been agreed upon by the True Whig leadership in advance of the convention. In the selection of representatives from the interior counties, the "conventions" frequently consist of informal gatherings of leading chiefs, influential Americo-Liberians who have farms in the counties, and representatives of the Department of Internal Affairs who decide upon "safe candidates." Unfortunately for the tribal people included within the newly drawn boundaries of the coastal counties in 1964 (at the time that the county sys-

tem was extended throughout the Republic), their influence is even less than that of their kinsmen in the hinterland. For, in the same year, Tubman announced that the
traditional practice of dividing the Senate seats within
each of the coastal counties between the towns and the less
developed areas would be abandoned.

The third circle of involvement consists for the most
part of those who hold or have held important posts in the
government of Liberia. This is the main bulwark of the
True Whig Party and of the Americo-Liberian class, even
though access is permitted to some few not born into the
class. This group tends to monopolize civic deference, and
entry into the circle is indicated by the title "Honorable"
on public occasions or in the local press. Another outward
and visible sign is the "knighting" of outstanding citizens
by the President, a practice initiated by Anthony Gardiner
in 1879 with the establishment of the Humane Order of
African Redemption. The most recent addition to these
odd trappings for a republic was Tubman's creation in
1955 of the Most Venerable Order of Knighthood of the
Pioneers of Liberia.

Holding office is not merely important for prestige. Public office provides access to the important sources of patronage: government jobs for one's relatives, attorney's
fees for representing the government in cases and contracts, the "forgiveness" of taxes and payments for services
of government, and the payment of a "dash" by any citizen
who receives a service or favor from a public official. Even
more significant forms of patronage, however, have appeared in the postwar period of economic growth. Free
housing and automobiles, frequent trips abroad on government business, preference in the awarding of foreign

scholarships, access to the President's favor in the acquisition of land in the tribal hinterland, and the privilege of receiving exorbitant tax-free rentals on private buildings leased by the government are all part of the patronage system that enables the Americo-Liberian class to maintain a higher standard of living than the tribal majority.

Passage from the outermost to the next circle of political involvement is essentially a transition in culture. It indicates movement from a circle in which the majority of individuals are still largely committed to tribal loyalties and traditional norms to a circle dominated by those who have accepted the cultural standards and the political, economic, and social structures of the Americo-Liberian community. Passage from the second to the third circle, however, is based upon much more narrowly ascriptive grounds. Participation in the third circle is monopolized largely by those identified by birth, marriage, or life style with the nineteenth-century pioneer founders of the Liberian state.

The Significance of Family Ties

The significance of the extended family in the politics of the tribal societies of Liberia has been dealt with in Chapter 2. Only suggestions have been given in the ethnographic and historical literature on Liberia with respect to the importance of the family as a political, economic, and social institution within the more Westernized sector of the population. Indeed, it is my contention that an understanding of family ties among the Americo-Liberian class is crucial to the understanding of the political system. An Americo-Liberian attaches great importance not only to the bilateral ties that he acquires at birth, but also to those he later acquires through his own marriage or even the marriage of his siblings and his children. Through birth or marriage he or she becomes a member of a series of corporate groups that impose obligations but also provide political allies in times of crisis or advance one's standing in the community. Family allies, moreover, provide information regarding changes in the political climate and access to the spoils available to the True Whig leadership.

Detailed knowledge of his own ties and the family ties of others is a *sine qua non* for the social and political survival of the individual. Birth and marriage are political events as much as they are social or economic ones and establish broader bonds than those among two or more individuals. Americo-Liberians interact not as individual personalities but as representatives of family groupings. On the basis of the affiliations of an acquaintance, one cultivates his friendship, shuns his company, or regards him as a political neutral. Knowledge of family ties also plays a peculiar role in maintaining the supremacy of the nontribal over the tribal community. Only occasionally is entry to the Americo-Liberian ruling class permitted to naturalized Liberians and to Gola, Grebo, and others who have undergone a measure of acculturation. The self-conscious efforts of late to publicize "mixed" marriages only serves to emphasize the exceptional character of the act.

Romantic love is certainly a factor both in marriage and in the establishment of informal liaisons. Marriages within the "honorable" class are not arranged in the Oriental manner. Nevertheless, an examination of the genealogies of the leading personalities of the political hierarchy in Liberia shows that connubial ties constitute an important element in the political advancement of the ambitious individual. Although a certain amount of permissiveness across class lines is tolerated in premarital and extramarital situations, the marriages of an "honorable" and of his siblings and children provide political alliances undertaken with an eye to the future. Thus, when the son of a cabinet member marries the daughter of a Senator or an ambassador, he is assured two patrons who will be concerned with his political advancement. The corollary to this situation is that divorce and remarriage are as much instruments of political realignment as they are of social readjustment. There is a strong correlation between the severance of marriage ties and the decline in the political fortunes of the family of one of the parties concerned. Divorce has become a normal weapon of group conflict, and the "sequential monogamy" practiced by many of the leading political personalities bears a rough approximation to the rise and fall in the political fortunes of the families of past, present, and prospective marriage partners.

An analysis of the genealogies of the political leadership of Liberia over a period of years provides the objective observer as well as the active participant with an explicit map of the Liberian political terrain, plotting not only the immediate strength of a given family and its patrons but also a history of the upward and downward movement of various families in the political scene. A political genealogy for 1960–1961, for example, indicated that there were three primary pockets of national strength, each dominated by a dominant patron: President William V.S. Tubman, Vice-President William R. Tolbert, and Secretary of the Treasury Charles B. Sherman.[2] In the case of the first two, a sig-

[2] *African One-Party States* (Ithaca, N.Y.: Cornell University Press, 1962), p. 369.

nificant link was forged in 1961 with the marriage of William V.S. Tubman, Jr., to Wokie Rose Tolbert, the daughter of the Vice-President. By 1968, however, the Cape Mount Shermans (as opposed to the Grand Bassa Shermans) were noticeably absent from the roster of the political elite, and they seemed destined to join the ranks of the Cassells, Colemans, and others whose political fortunes had waxed and then waned during earlier stages of the Tubman presidency. By 1968, President Tubman was more firmly entrenched than ever (see Chart 1). A cluster of his own relatives (the Barnes, Yancy, and Brewer families of Maryland County) and his wife's (the Padmore, Grimes, Wiles, and other families associated with the Barclays) dominated the executive, legislative, and judicial branches of government and controlled a good portion of the diplomatic posts as well. Although the Tolbert group had been affected by the removal of Stephen Tolbert to a position of influence outside the formal government apparatus, it remained strongly entrenched in a number of key financial offices. Similarly well placed in the area of finance and economic planning were the relatives of Richard S. S. Bright, a former diplomat who had used his political influence to acquire a considerable share of the independent rubber market. Scattered throughout the accompanying chart on family and politics are representatives of families that have always played a substantial role in Liberian politics (the various branches of the Cooper, Dennis, and Gibson families) as well as smaller families whose influence is on the rise or decline. Space does not permit me to include several very significant new family clusters that have been gathering strength during the past decade: the relatives of Postmaster-General McKinley DeShield, Sec-

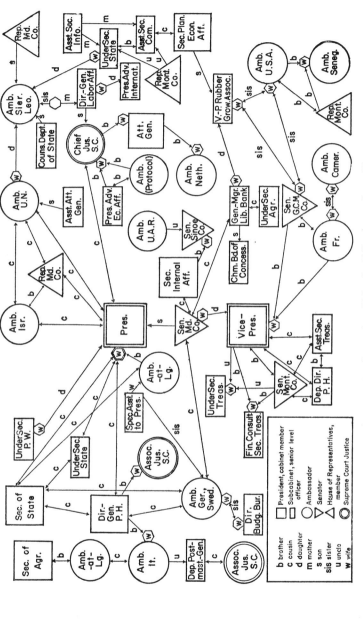

Chart 1. Family and politics in Liberia, 1967–1968

retary of the Treasury James Milton Weeks, and Speaker of the House Richard A. Henries, for example.

Perhaps the family with the greatest resilience on the national scene are the descendants of Arthur Barclay, who emigrated to Liberia from the West Indies in 1865 and became the Republic's fifteenth President. His heirs have included two Presidents, several Justices of the Supreme Court, and a host of diplomats, legislators and cabinet members. Mrs. Tubman, the present Secretary of State, the Director of the National Public Health Service, and a recent ambassador to the United States are all members of the Barclay clan. Regionally, certain families such as the Grigsbys in Sinoe, the Morgans in Grand Bassa, or the Gibsons in Maryland have greater prominence than others and tend to monopolize elective and appointive posts within their respective counties. Several families, on the other hand, enjoy national pre-eminence. These include not only the leading families of Monrovia or Montserrado County, such as the Barclays, the Grimes, and the Kings, but also the Tubmans of Maryland and the Sherman and Freeman families of Cape Mount.

The recruitment of one's kinsmen to office provides the Whig patron with increased status within the party as well as greater access to other forms of patronage. It is, however, a double-edged sword, for it increases the vulnerability of the key patron vis-à-vis other family leaders and the President himself. The possibilities of a minor member of the clan committing an indiscretion that embarrasses the key patron are great. The position of the President, too, is considerably enhanced by his role as the indispensable arbiter of interfamily conflicts. He can, moreover, put a major challenger to presidential authority "on notice" indirectly by removing some of his lesser kinsmen from office. In this way, the equilibrium so essential to the maintenance of Whig supremacy is not greatly disturbed.

New Entrants to the "Honorable" Class

While leadership in the third circle of influence is derived primarily from those who have links with the early settlers of Liberia, it is apparent that new blood is added from time to time from the lower ranks of the Americo-Liberian community, from Negro immigration from the New World or neighboring African states, and from the tribal sector of the Liberian population itself. Indeed, even prior to Tubman the exclusion of the indigenous population from power was far from total. There were at least three ways in which persons of tribal origin could be accepted as members of the "honorable" class. For example, under the "ward" system, talented tribal youths who have been given to prominent Americo-Liberian families for care and training have found one avenue to cultural assimilation. Although there have been instances of abuse in which the ward differs only slightly from a domestic servant, there have also been countless cases in which tribal youths have been adopted in the fullest sense and given all the privileges of education and access to politics afforded a full-fledged Americo-Liberian youth. One of the present members of the Legislature is a tribal ward of former President Edwin Barclay.

A second precursor of Tubman's Unification Policy is found in the liaisons that Americo-Liberian males (and occasionally females) have established with tribal persons, frequently without benefit of clergy. Fortunately for the offspring of such unions, neither illegitimacy nor the mixed character of one's parentage has such stigma attached to it in Liberia. Indeed, several of the loading members of Tubman's cabinet and of the ambassadorial group find it advantageous to stress the tribal backgrounds of their parents, and at least one is even quite proud of the fact that he is a "wild oat."

A third form of assimilation of tribal persons into the Americo-Liberian elite has come through co-optation of leading tribal personalities who were instrumental in establishing Liberian authority in their respective areas during the past century and a half. These tribal leaders have shared in the patronage available to Americo-Liberians, have gained prominent posts in government, and have had their children educated abroad. Although it has been politically expedient for these individuals to maintain their traditional connections, for all practical purposes they have accepted the settler culture. The Mandingo tribesmen deserve special mention since they have been made an auxiliary of the Americo-Liberian community despite their early opposition to settler expansion into the interior. Their talent in commercial enterprises has been appreciated by President Tubman, who has encouraged them to emigrate from Guinea and other West African states. They enjoy exemption from compulsory tribal labor, and they are not normally subject to the jurisdiction of tribal courts.

In addition to accretions from the tribal ranks, the Americo-Liberian community during the past hundred years has had a small but steady infusion of new blood from other African countries, the West Indies, and the United States. Liberian governments have blown hot and cold toward Negro immigration from the United States.

The immigrants, who are frequently better educated and accustomed to more modern amenities, have tended to be hypercritical of conditions in Liberia. Frequently, for them residence in Liberia is a temporary matter, and they often become disillusioned with affairs and move to one of the newer African states or return to the New World. Some of the fears currently held by the Americo-Liberians were revealed in October, 1967, when a special commission was established to supervise the settlement of new immigrants. At a presidential news conference, Tubman indicated quite pointedly that the immigrant community from the New World should not be too large to be integrated into the existing framework of society. He noted further—with obvious reference to potential Black Muslim and Black Power immigrants—that Liberia would not tolerate any racial hatred or animosity, and that it would require the immigrants to pledge themselves to uphold the principle of separation of church and state.[3] Although my genealogical charts indicated a number of West Indian Negro males who had attained fairly high political office, I was unable to locate any American Negro male immigrants in the upper reaches of the political hierarchy. Many of the Americo-Liberian officials, however, were married to American Negro wives. It is highly significant that in 1962 the census takers identified only 231 of the 10,268 citizens of foreign birth as coming from the United States. The majority of new citizens came from Guinea

[3] *West Africa,* 7 Oct. 1967. During Vice-President Hubert Humphrey's visit to Liberia in 1968, he greeted leaders of a group of 160 Negro "Hebrews" who had settled at Ghabartella, 50 miles inland from Monrovia. They had recently emigrated from Chicago and regarded themselves as children of Israel who had come home.

(4,469), Sierra Leone (2,601), Ghana (1,359), and the Ivory Coast (754).

Under the Tubman regime the elevation of persons of tribal origins and persons from the lower strata of the Americo-Liberian society into the "honorable" class has been remarkably accelerated. The expansion of the bureaucracy to cope with the vast economic changes and the creation of diplomatic posts in various quarters of the globe have placed a marked strain upon the limited pool of talent available from the list of the top fifteen or twenty families. The lack of French-speaking Americo-Liberians, for example, has led the regime to recruit young, educated tribal persons whose homes are near the Guinean or Ivory Coast border for assignment to Liberian embassies in Haiti or the French-speaking countries of Africa. In a society increasingly concerned with technology, moreover, excellent performance in a skill may bring an educated tribal youth to the attention of the President or a leading politician who will serve as the young man's "patron." Other talents, such as a gift for oratory—so characteristic of the Liberian political style—may be a prime factor in the political advancement of a tribal youth or a poorer Americo-Liberian who is eager to leave his profession as a teacher or preacher.

Those who advance on the basis of merit alone or in spite of their tribal or alien background constitute potential threats to the regime. Advancement from outside the third circle constitutes not only an attack upon the rules of political preferment but also invites the possibility of the new entrant's gaining a following among the tribal majority. This accounts for the early and occasionally ruthless political demise of officials who have unduly emphasized their tribal antecedents and as a consequence achieved a mass appeal. Three cabinet members during the past few years have suffered such a fate. The threat posed by the new entrant diminishes if he is "legitimized" by the establishment of marriage ties with the leading families. This is obviously of value to him. It also helps maintain the system, for he acquires a vested interest in the preservation of the privileged status of the ruling group, as well as a group of in-laws who will attempt to ensure that his adopted loyalties take precedence over his loyalties to his former tribe, kinsmen, or country.

The Cores of Influence

In analyzing the characteristics of the Whig Party leadership that stands at the fourth circle of political involvement—the actual officeholders—one is struck by the emphasis on more than family ties. As a group the present generation of Liberian officials have had a greater per capita exposure to higher education than most of the leadership groups in the newer African states. The establishment of Liberia College (now the University of Liberia) around 1858–1862 gave Liberia a considerable educational lead over its neighbors. Its advantage in university graduates has been supplemented in the postwar period by the establishment of Cuttington College in the interior and Our Lady of Fatima College in Maryland as well as by a veritable exodus of Liberian youths to study in the United States, Western Europe, Israel, and Asia under missionary, American government, and other types of scholarships. Although Tubman did not receive a university education, his use of the title "Doctor" indicates the high value placed upon even an honorary degree from the

University of Liberia. Over two-thirds of the officials holding cabinet or subcabinet rank have at least one college degree, and roughly half of this group have received some higher education abroad.

One is impressed, too, with the youth of those holding key government posts. Admittedly, many of the Old Guard continue to exercise influence in the party behind the scenes. Inevitably, however, the occupants of government offices tend to monopolize patronage and hence power within the party. In 1962 the cabinet members in charge of the Departments of State, National Defense, Education, National Public Health Service, Public Works and Utilities, and Justice ranged between thirty and forty-two years of age. In 1968 the average age of the new cabinet was the lowest in this century. The same youth and vitality is evident in the diplomatic personnel now being dispatched to the four corners of the globe to represent Liberia's growing economic and political interests.

Finally, as was suggested in Chapter 5, the innermost circle is characterized by a high degree of full-time commitment to politics. There is a decided antipathy or disdain for commerce and agriculture; involvement in business and agriculture is only a by-product of a political career. The reverse is seldom the case. The preference for politics and the law is clearly reflected in the degrees received by Liberian students at home and abroad and in the almost immediate pursuit of political office even by those whose scholarships compelled them to take technical courses of education.

It is at the core of political involvement, the innermost circle, that we discover the real key to the future direction and tempo of change. For at the center of all things political in Liberia stands the President. Under Tubman the institution has undergone a remarkable transformation with the previous bases for presidential authority being irretrievably altered. Much depends upon the longevity and political acumen of President Tubman or the qualities of his successor in determining whether the pendulum of political power in Liberia will ultimately swing in favor of the tribal majority.

CHAPTER 8

The Cult of
the Presidency

The subordination of economic and other interests to politics, the True Whig Party's monopoly of the electoral system, and the reliance upon family ties as an instrument of political recruitment have served as effective mechanisms in maintaining the supremacy of the Americo-Liberian community in a changing Liberia. The ultimate line of defense in preserving an island of privilege in a sea of hostility, however, has been the emergence of a strong presidency. While the presidency continues to serve as a guardian of privilege, however, it has also become under William Tubman the most dynamic factor in determining the pace, character, and direction of change. Tubman's predecessors defended the *status quo* by resisting change. Tubman prefers to manipulate the champions of the *status quo* in making a positive response to inevitable demands for change.

Tubman's long tenure in office gives him an advantage over his predecessors in terms of making a significant impact upon the office. Tenure alone, however, cannot explain the dramatic changes in the institution since Tubman assumed office in 1944. His remarkable personality, his full knowledge of even the most minor detail of the political terrain, his pursuit of imaginative policies in the face of a wall of opposition on the part of the Old Guard, and his ability to disguise tactical retreats as victories are all part of the story. Most important, he is the first Chief Executive of Liberia who has attempted to be the President of Liberia instead of merely the servant of the Americo-Liberian community.

The emergence of the President as the dominant figure in Liberian national politics, with the consequent subordination of the other two major branches of the national government, was neither desired nor anticipated by the founding fathers of the Republic. Indeed, despite the long tenures of Joseph Jenkins Roberts (1848–1856, 1872–1876), Hilary Johnson (1884–1892), and other strong-willed presidents during the first fifty years of independence, this pattern did not crystallize until well into the present century. In fact, until the 1930's precedent suggested the contrary. Of the seventeen men who have held the office during nineteen presidencies (two were elected for second, nonconsecutive terms), only seven (Benson, Roberts in 1876, Johnson, Gibson, Arthur Barclay, Howard, and Edwin Barclay) retired voluntarily. In an eighth case (Cheeseman) the President died in office. Excluding the present incumbent, of the ten remaining Presidents, four (Roberts in 1855, Warner, and Payne in both 1869 and 1877) were defeated in their bids for reelection; one (Russell) lost the support of his party and was not renominated; one (Roye) was forcibly deposed; three (Gardiner, Coleman, and King) were compelled to resign under the implied or explicit threat of impeachment, and one succeeding vice-president (Smith) was forced to accept a truncated term of several months until a new election could be held. In addition to the ten who lost power, at least one more—Garretson Gibson—was threatened by a mob calling for his resignation. He failed, however, to panic.

The Growth of Presidential Power

A number of factors account for this recent growth in the powers of the President. Partly it is the result of a series of constitutional amendments to the 1847 provision that required the President to seek reelection every two years. Now, following an initial term of eight years, a President may run for any successive number of four-year terms. This has not only freed the executive from recurrent intraparty struggles and campaigning, but it also permits him to launch long-range programs and to consolidate a personal following in the various branches of government. The President, too, has been one of the prime beneficiaries of the increasing effectiveness of the central government's administrative and military services and the improvement in transportation and communications: The regional appointees of the President are increasingly subject to his control. An elaborate system of surveillance, including the employment of "personal relations officers" who report directly to the President, *ad hoc* reviews of specific situations by the President or one of his subordinates, and the penchant of the present Chief Executive to scrutinize vouchers of more than $250 have also strengthened the President's hand in the political system.

The expanding dimension of governmental operation in Liberia as a result of foreign investment and United States government aid has also been a significant factor. In a country where few offices are elective, the civil service system exists largely on paper, and where the government is one of the largest employers of personnel, the power of appointment provides the president with a powerful political weapon. The expansion of governmental operations means not only more jobs to distribute but also more perquisites of office that can be dispensed to reward the faithful, seduce the doubtful, and entrap the powerful opponents of the regime. Moreover, in a country in which the extended family is an important political group, the executive does not limit the use of patronage to entrenchment of his own family. He uses patronage to keep the leading families in a state of equilibrium so that no single group constitutes a threat. This accounts for the "rapidly changing face" of the bureaucracy. When one contender and his family appear to be gaining patronage and prestige, the family is actually increasing its vulnerability with respect to the President and other leading families. In this situation the President is indispensable as the arbiter of interdynastic disputes.

The Presidency under Tubman

The presidency has become an indispensable institution in still another crucial respect. The external and internal threats posed to Americo-Liberian supremacy in the Republic have forced the settler group to accept the solitary leadership of the President rather than that of the pluralistic and locally oriented legislature. Indeed, the resignations of Presidents King (1930), Coleman (1900), and Gardiner (1883) were forced precisely because the incumbent President's actions exposed the settler community to foreign or tribal enemies. The critical importance of the President to the Americo-Liberian community has become even more apparent during the administration of Tubman. Tubman has felt compelled to emulate some of his West

African neighbors by casting himself in the role of a charismatic leader who can breach the social and tribal schisms within Liberia. There is little doubt that he has had greater popularity with the tribal people than any President before him. His accessibility and dispensation of personal justice, his respect for tribal customs, the ceremonial aspects of his Unification Policy, and his informality on public occasions have had a decided appeal to the indigenous element. It is questionable whether these things justify the erection of statues of Tubman around the country or whether they are sufficient to offset some of the obvious deficiencies of the Unification Policy. Nevertheless, there is no other Americo-Liberian who has as popular a following among the tribal people, and tribal challengers to the President's leadership have been effectively removed from active politics. Thus, no other leader on the scene today could satisfy both communities.

Despite Tubman's announcement in January, 1968, that this term in office (his sixth) would be his last, few people in Liberia really took him seriously. Indeed, he made similar statements in 1964, 1960, 1956, and 1952. There are many individuals, no doubt, who would like the job, but few on the scene today could match Tubman's broad base of support. The Americo-Liberians, for example, appreciate that their initial fears regarding the Open-Door Policy have not as yet materialized. The policy has yielded considerable financial benefits for the elite without unduly mobilizing the tribal people in political terms. The descendants of the settlers appreciate, too, that Tubman's approach to international politics has thus far shielded Liberia from the pressures of African nationalism.

While he is the dominant figure in Liberian national politics, the President is not a dictator. A more accurate description would be that he has been the presiding officer of the America-Liberian ruling class and that increasingly, under Tubman, the President has become the managing director of a moderate social revolution. Although he may manipulate the leadership of various family, regional, tribal, and other groups, he also depends upon them for support. The continuing problems of transportation and communication and the inefficiencies of administration (especially with respect to postaudits) leave many independent pockets of political power throughout the system. The relative political autonomy of these groups forces the President constantly to placate his political opposition. The hand of forgiveness is always extended, and even those removed from office on serious charges or imprisoned for grievous offenses find that the gates of patronage are never completely closed. With luck, after a due period of grace, the penitent may be appointed to an even higher post in government. The President cannot rely too strongly on his personal popularity as a weapon with which to control the political opposition. The insecurity of Tubman's charisma is certainly evidenced by the fact that much of what passes for expressions of popular support is either highly subsidized by government or is the result of legal and unofficial coercion. Any unpopularity is masked by the absence of an independent press and by the severity of the libel, slander, and sedition laws when it comes to criticism of the President or his family.[1]

Adulation of The Presidency

Government subsidization of the adulation of the President is everywhere, in the erection of his statues at various points in the country; the naming of bridges, streets, and

[1] *Liberian Code of Laws of 1956,* title 27, ch. 3, secs. 52–57.

public buildings after the President, his wife, or his mother; the requirement that Tubman's picture be displayed in every commercial establishment; and the observance of public holidays to commemorate significant events in his life—such as the failure of the assassination attempt of 1955. At times the claque that precedes him on every public occasion borders on blasphemy in its attempt to emphasize the extraordinary character of the Tubman personality. The *Liberian Age,* too, frequently publishes such contributions from its readers as the "Ten Commandments of Tubmanism," and its own reporters dutifully reported that during one of Tubman's appearances, "blue heaven sent a light shower of blessing upon the partisans." [2] The adulation extends occasionally to Mrs. Tubman, who was greeted upon her return from a trip to Europe in 1960 by a huge banner in downtown Monrovia proclaiming: "Welcome Back Our Blessed Lady Antoinette."

Criticism of the high cost of presidential adulation is mounting. One of the more onerous aspects is the recurrent annual deduction made from the salaries of teachers and other public employees to provide a more spectacular birthday present for Tubman every November 29th. In 1959 the celebrations were still of manageable proportions, with a few thousand citizens and foreigners attending a picnic given in the President's honor by Vice-President Tolbert. The next year the President was presented with a new car, the following year a yacht, then a plane, and finally a series of public buildings: a library, a cultural center, and then a military academy. The site of the birthday celebrations rotates around the country, and

[2] 12 Aug. 1960, p. 3; 6 May 1960, p. 11.

each county vies to outdo the others. The only people who suffer are the public employees, who once again find their monthly paychecks depleted.[3]

The greatest single example of presidential adulation is the new Executive Mansion. Perhaps it was time that the Liberian government owned an Executive Mansion, for the previous one—like most public buildings in Liberia, including schools—was "rented" to the government by the "honorable" family that owned it. Nevertheless, for a government with an annual budget of $27,000,000 in 1960, it was somewhat questionable whether the country could afford one building that ultimately cost around $15,000,-000. The President's instructions to the architect were simple: "It should be awesome." When faced with criticism, Tubman responded: "It is too fabulous for a country with economic and financial resources such as ours. . . . It is too good for me to live in, but not too good for a President of Liberia." [4]

Recruitment for the Presidency

The editorial question posed to Tubman in the August 15, 1960 issue of the *Liberian Age*—"Who Are You Grooming for the Presidency?"—remained unanswered as Tubman began his sixth term in office in 1968. Perhaps the question cannot be safely answered. Even in a highly democratic society, a chief executive rarely encourages competition for his mantle. There is the real possibility of a shift of influence before the incumbent is prepared to sacrifice his power. An examination of the critical role the

[3] Cf. Albert Porte, "The Observance of President Tubman's Birthday in Liberia," Monrovia, October 1965, mimeographed.

[4] *West Africa,* 26 Oct. 1963.

presidency plays in balancing the various forces within the Liberian political system makes it quite clear that presidential authority is not divisible. This is a lesson that ex-Presidents Arthur Barclay, Daniel Howard, and Charles D. B. King learned to their sorrow as they failed to control the actions of their successors.

The style of Liberian politics seldom permits the question of succession to be raised. It is assumed that a President will attempt to succeed himself even when the constitution seems to deny him this privilege—as it did during Edwin Barclay's second term and William Tubman's first term. From the outset of his term of office, the incumbent is besieged with resolutions from local chapters of the True Whig Party urging him to seek reelection. Indeed, the first resolution urging Tubman to run for a fifth term came two weeks after his renomination by the party convention in 1959 for a fourth term.[5] Already he has received a petition from the Women's Branch of the party asking him to stand for a seventh term in 1972.

Despite his remarkable vitality, it is possible that death, ill health (he had his seventy-third birthday in 1968 and spent two months during the previous year on medical leave in Switzerland), or even a political disturbance could compel the True Whig Party to consider a successor to Tubman in the very near future. Constitutionally, Vice-President William Tolbert is next in line. On three occasions in Liberian history (1871, 1900, and 1930), however, the constitutional successor in a time of crisis was bypassed in favor of one more acceptable to the dominant political forces of the day. Tolbert's problem is whether he fits the image of the presidency constructed by Tubman under his

[5] *Daily Listener,* 10 Feb. 1959, p. 1.

Unification Policy. The Tubman image differs radically from the one erected by his predecessors. To maintain the present political system, the President must be acceptable to both the Americo-Liberians and the tribal element without being too closely identified with the primary interests of either one. He must have the appreciation of pomp and ceremony that the aristocratic-minded Whigs demand of their leader and yet have the human foibles—indeed, the ability to act the clown—that has enhanced Tubman's reputation with the tribal masses. William Tolbert does not fit the Tubman image, for his appeal has been largely to the Americo-Liberian elite. Indeed, both his brothers are reputed to have greater influence than he has among the Americo-Liberian group.

Private speculation about long-term successors previously centered upon the former Secretary of the Treasury, Charles Sherman, whose presidential ambitions were well known to Tubman. Sherman undoubtedly has one of the keenest minds in Liberia. His credentials among Americo-Liberians are solid, for his father, General Reginald A. Sherman, several times saved the settlers from defeat at the hands of tribal rebels. On the other hand, Sherman does not conceal the fact that his mother was a tribal woman. He and other younger men, such as Secretary of State Rudolph Grimes, have attempted to stress their tribal antecedents or concern with the lot of the tribal people while maintaining the correct posture with their fellow Americo-Liberians.

Inevitably, discussion turns to the future of "Shad, Jr.," President Tubman's son by an earlier marriage, whom Tubman, Sr., made Chief of the Cabinet in 1964 and later Senator from Maryland County, a post once held by Tub-

man, Sr. "Shad, Jr." has both youth and an American education at both Harvard and Rutgers. Prior to holding public office, moreover, he served as president general of the
Labor Congress of Industrial Organization and thereby
became identified (as his father had before him) with the
lot of those who pose the greatest threat to Whig supremacy: the lower-middle classes and the tribalized elements of
Monrovia. With success he may build the popular image
that his father did years ago as an attorney in Maryland
County when he took without fee the cases of the destitute.
Shad, Jr., has used his position to advantage in speaking
before civic clubs or at school exercises. His recurrent
theme is that the enemy of the working class is not the
True Whig Party leadership, but rather the Lebanese and
other foreign entrepreneurs in Liberia.[6] His marriage to
the daughter of Vice-President Tolbert in 1961 was taken
by several observers to indicate that Tolbert's possible succession would constitute a mere holding operation for
Tubman's son.

The Significance of the Legislature

In the furtherance of many Whig objectives the Speaker
of the House, the president pro tempore of the Senate, and
other leading legislators may personally exercise considerably greater influence over the course of affairs than members of the President's cabinet. As an institution, however,
the Legislature has been decidedly eclipsed by the presidency. This subordination has been especially apparent
during the administrations of Edwin Barclay (1930–
1944) and his successor, William Tubman. None of the
author's informants could point to one significant measure

[6] *Ibid.*, 2 July 1962, p. 3.

that had emerged from the Legislature without presidential approval, nor could they point to any major legislation that failed in the face of concerted and sustained support from the Executive Mansion.

This does not mean that the House and the Senate are completely under the domination of the President, for the membership of the Legislature includes some of the leading figures in the hierarchy of the True Whig Party. These men have bases of political support that are independent of the President. The Speaker of the House, the Vice-President, the president pro tempore of the Senate, as well as the senior men in the county delegations, are powerful figures within their own areas. Consultation behind the scene and surveying the opposition in advance are required to spare the President public political defeat. The President gets his way eventually and substantially, if not always completely or immediately, on every measure he introduces. Senators or representatives are permitted to place a personal imprint upon certain types of legislation and even to object to the passage of a measure.

The expression of legislative independence, however is often illusory. Delay in passage of a bill may actually indicate the lack of presidential intent to do more than publicly espouse a reform that he has no intention of putting into effect at that time. Similarly the senatorial rejection of a presidential nomination for the Supreme Court may create an impression of legislative independence. The only recent case, however, was openly acknowledged as a façade for a change of heart on the part of the President himself. The Senator who led the assault on the presidential nominee was himself immediately nominated for the same post. The subordinate role of the Legislature was clearly expressed in the remarks of the Vice-President to this writer in 1960 at the opening of the Legislature. Mr. Tolbert stated that the House and the Senate could not consider any measure during the first month inasmuch as the President was still in Europe and "we don't know what his thoughts are." Significantly, the $27,000,000 annual budget introduced on December 23, 1960, was passed into law on the following day, without amendment.

Although as a body the Legislature does not initiate legislation or provide a public check upon presidential power, it does have an educative function to perform. Its debates are lively, if highly rhetorical, and help to educate the local leadership and the general public regarding the significance of a new policy decision. The debates often expose defects or pitfalls in a proposed measure, which helps the executive branch in reformulating its proposal and the drafting committees of the Legislature in presenting a final version of the measure.

The Legislature's representative function is poorly served by the tendency to make decisions outside the legislative body and by the policy of the True Whig Party to derogate pressure-group activity to a minor role in the political process. Party representation, moreover, exaggerates the strength of the True Whig Party, which has enjoyed a virtual monopoly in the Legislature since the founding of the party.

Despite the lack of significant power in the matter of legislation, the office of Senator or Representative is eagerly sought. Membership in the Legislature automatically gives one the title of "Honorable" as well as the perquisites due to the very few elective officials in Liberia. In addition to the other forms of patronage available to party members in good standing, a high proportion of the legislators receive attorney's fees for representing the foreign concessionaires and the more prominent private Liberians. Speaker of the House Richard Henries, for example, has the most flourishing law practice in the country. If he is not a lawyer at the time of election, the fledgling legislator quickly finds himself studying for the bar. The Legislature, moreover, is regarded as a very attractive forum for the establishment of a national reputation. With success a young man may go on to the Supreme Court, an ambassadorship, the cabinet, or even as high as the Presidency. In any case, the two-term tradition of the True Whig Party assures the Senator at the end of six years and the Representative at the end of four years that his term of office will be renewed largely without a contest. Some have been able to extend their tenure indefinitely. Legislators, too, may feel that their regional and family alliances give them independent bases for political support and may challenge the President. A recent example was the Senate's objections to various provisions in the proposed Mount Coffee Hydro Agreement.[7]

The Judiciary

The judiciary is very much the third branch of the national government. Despite the constitutional provision upholding the independence of the judiciary, the judges of the Supreme Court and subordinate courts are in fact subject to the control of the other two branches of the government. The removal of judges by joint resolution of the Legislature is a fairly common occurrence. Two Justices of the Supreme Court, for example, were removed in 1957.

[7] *Liberian Age,* 21 Dec. 1962, p. 2.

The occasional display of independence by the judiciary is treated with indifference by the more obviously political branches. A case in point was the classic decision of 1919 in which the Court declared that the existing system of administration in the interior was unconstitutional: that pattern of administration continued to 1964.

The lack of prior judicial experience or even legal training is apparent at all levels of the court system. Chief Justice A. Dash Wilson, upon taking office in 1958, delivered a caustic lecture to the whole judiciary that noted the persistent bias on the part of the judges with respect to litigants, the many improper instructions to juries, and the lack of courage on the part of the courts in dealing with unscrupulous lawyers. In 1966 the Chief Justice announced that the collection of fines, costs, and fees by judges and clerks of the court had resulted in such a flagrant distortion of justice that judges were required to turn this function over to administrative officers.

Perhaps the greatest problem concerning the judiciary is the delay in bringing cases to completion. The first judicial circuit of Montserrado County in 1960, for example, was able to dispose of less than 7 per cent of the 1,297 criminal cases on its dockets.[8] Similar situations prevailed in the other tribunals, especially those dealing with civil cases. For a community that places a high value on litigation, this is indeed a serious problem. Litigation, in fact, is one of the most effective weapons for keeping the politically and socially diffident Liberians in line. The expense, the loss of business time, the neglect of his family and friends, as well as other byproducts of protracted court

[8] Republic of Liberia, "Annual Report of the Attorney General," 1959–1960, App. B; *Liberian Age,* 31 March 1958, p. 4.

cases dampen the enthusiasm of the social mischief-maker and the political reformer.[9]

Control Over the Bureaucracy

Supremacy of the presidency in the national government has come not merely through the subordination of the other two major branches; it is equally a consequence of increased presidential control over the bureaucracy. Presidential control, however, has not meant greater administrative efficiency. As the central government expands its agencies throughout the Republic, the failure of the national government to address itself to the problems of the civil service becomes increasingly apparent. Indeed, administrative inefficiency and dishonesty undermine the very system of control the Americo-Liberians are attempting to expand and perpetuate.

In theory the Republic of Liberia is a highly centralized unitary state. There is relatively little legal autonomy enjoyed by the major political subdivisions—the five coastal and four interior counties—or by the districts, territories, and municipalities into which the counties are subdivided.[10] In fact, only the counties and municipalities have a basis in the constitution, whereas the other units remain creatures of the Legislature. Administrative officials at all levels are appointed by the President or by the President with the advice and consent of the Senate. Decisions regarding policies, programs, and the expenditure of funds

[9] See Parker, "Acculturation in Liberia," p. 270.

[10] Prior to 1964 the hinterland area was divided into three provinces under provincial commissioners. In 1964 the boundaries of the coastal counties were extended inland prior to the establishment of the four new interior counties.

are also largely at the national level. Revenue collection, moreover, is virtually a monopoly of the central government, even though the fines and fees collected by chiefs may be spent for local projects under proper central government supervision. The political division of the country tends largely to be disregarded by the departments of the national government in the planning of programs in agriculture, health, education, and other fields. Thus, the superintendents of counties and territories and the district commissioners are "chief executives" of their respective areas in only a limited number of government functions. The counties and territories exist largely as electoral areas for the national legislature or, together with the hinterland and coastal districts, as units for the maintenance of order and the collection of taxes.

Unfortunately for the theory of administrative organization, a number of factors have militated against the assertion of central government authority in many areas of the Republic. Most significant are the geographical barriers to an inexpensive and effective system of transport and communications, the emergence of satrapies along the coastal strip under the control of leading families, the resistance of the tribal people, and the historic trepidation or indifference of the Americo-Liberians to the establishment of control over the hinterland. As a consequence of these things, in many areas of the Republic little gets done by way of positive governmental programs or what is done is accomplished in a highly inefficient manner with a maximum amount of coercion from the top and scant initiative or enthusiasm at the grass-roots level.

New highways, the airplane, and the radio provide the means for centralizing administrative control over field services. Much more has to be done, however, to improve the system of public administration at both national and local levels. It does no good to hold the field officer responsible for implementing national government policy directives if he has almost no trained staff, is indifferent to the need for adequate reports and records, and has only sporadic supervision of his work by higher officials. Nor is central government direction feasible if the executive branch has only recently recognized the value of planning or data collection, if the President ignores the legal chain of command from chiefs up through the Secretary of Internal Affairs and insists upon being accessible to all, or if the President rigorously studies the preaudit expenditures but almost ignores postaudit. Indeed, all the problems of public administration both in developed states and in other African countries appear to be compounded in Liberia.

Perhaps the heart of the problem is personnel. In terms of per capita exposure to university training, the Liberian upper class is among the best educated of any African state. This would seem to give the government of Liberia a decided advantage over its neighbors. But this is not the case. Partly this results from the inadequacies of the education received at the University of Liberia or the smaller colleges of the United States. It is also a product of the overemphasis upon legal and political studies to the neglect of agriculture, engineering, accounting, business administration, and other subjects that form the substance of governmental programs or are essential to the efficient operation of government. Even if a Liberian student does pursue a technical course, however, there is no guarantee that his talents will be put to the best use. Sheer inefficiency in allocating personnel, the student's own recognition that politics will be the most rewarding profession in the long run, and the operation of the patronage system have all contributed to the waste of human talent by the government.

The patronage system pervades all administrative practices. Although in some instances appointment or promotion is based on merit rather than influence, this usually happens only when a particular skill is required in a hurry. As the civil service commissioners have testified in their annual reports, the senior executives regard with scorn such notions as the competitive testing and certification of candidates, the establishment of impartial criteria for the promotion or firing of employees, and the need for preservice or in-service training for posts in government. Only the Department of State has attempted to regularize its testing and training programs for foreign service officers and thereby reduce some—but certainly not all—of the evils of patronage. This effort attests to the critical importance attached by Liberia to good public relations in international politics.

In patronage terms the government employee has a dual obligation. The obligation to the President and the True Whig Party is satisfied by attendance at rallies, by voting, by public displays of loyalty to the President, and by the annual "contribution" to the True Whig Party, which is automatically deducted from his salary. The second obligation is to his patron or patrons, whom he supports in their struggle for power with other influential members of the political hierarchy, including perhaps the employee's administrative superiors. The spread of patronage ties, which are in many cases synonymous with blood and marriage ties, provides the President with a useful mechanism for maintaining control over the political system. There is a built-in watchdog system, with each bloc reporting the sins of omission and commission of the competing bloc. Patronage rivalry, however, takes its toll on administrative boldness in launching new programs and generally plays havoc with a superior's control of his subordinates. A simple executive directive may easily be converted into a contest for power at a higher level in the bureaucracy. The authorized lines of command are often jammed. Action frequently takes place only by means of circuitous communication, and the consequent delay is often fatal for programs.

In addition to its inefficiencies, the Liberian bureaucracy is clearly too large. The expansion of government into areas that might more efficiently be left to private hands is but one of the factors. The lack of planning, the inadequacies of training, and the cultural insistence upon a rigid division of labor also contribute to a multiplication of the number of workers required if administrative programs are to be accomplished at all. The expansion of the bureaucracy increases the need for the general service staff and contributes to a reduction in salary scales at the lower level, which in turn perpetuates the demand for "dash" or petty gifts in return for any service rendered by a public employee.

At the higher levels of the bureaucracy, the inadequacies of training are not so apparent. Although in 1961 several senior members of the government were only high-school graduates, by 1968 this had become the exception. A good many of them have advanced degrees from the best universities in America and Europe. Indeed, articulateness of

Liberian leaders regarding the problems of government is disarming to the outside observer, who later discovers a great chasm between the expressed desire for reform and any positive evidence that administrative and political energies are being directed toward that end. Some of the most vociferous critics of patronage stand at the heart of a vast patronage empire. On the slightest provocation, moreover, agency heads with major responsibilities for new programs undertake extended trips to visit community development schemes in the Negev Desert or clinics for midwives in the Soviet Union. Often the only time a senior official ventures into the interior of Liberia is to visit his rubber farm or to attend a ceremonial function. There is apparently no notion of a conflict of interest when a government official reaps personal financial profit from his position by securing a monopoly for his company or by receiving retaining fees from foreign concessions. Such behavior is not inconsistent with the moral standards of the nontribal element, and, indeed, it is compatible with the efforts of the ruling class to control economic development so that neither a tribal nor a settler middle class emerges to challenge the existing order. Whether it stimulates or inhibits rapid economic development is an arguable matter. It does compromise the official's objectivity, however, and detracts from the performance of his duties. Ultimately, it may have the unintended result of undermining the very social and political system it is designed to perpetuate.

To compensate for inadequacies of training and to overcome some inefficient practices, the Liberian government under President Tubman has placed increased reliance upon foreign advisers from the United States, Great Britain, Israel, and other developed countries. The American

Agency for International Development (and its predecessors) and United Nations specialized agencies have provided most of the external advisers. The fact that European and American financial and other advisers were imposed upon Liberia at various points in its recent past has made the task of the foreign adviser a difficult one indeed. Some advisers find the inertia and lack of cooperation too much to bear and quit in disgust. Others attempt to deal with their frustrations by assuming an operational rather than an advisory role. On the whole, the Liberian government usually does not get its money's worth from its foreign advisers, but it is not certain that the government intended to. In certain cases the foreign adviser is even made the unwitting scapegoat for the institution of a new program that encounters public opposition.

Many signs indicate that the President is finding it more and more difficult to control all phases of bureaucratic activity. The increasing frequency of either dismissal or rotation to new posts of fairly senior officers of the national government are evidence of a loss of trust between the Chief Executive and some of his major subordinates. The ability of the President and the cabinet to continue to control the character, pace, and direction of change is certainly being challenged by the increasing scope of governmental operations, not only on the domestic scene but in international affairs as well. Unless there is dramatic change in the entire philosophy of bureaucratic growth, the national administration will find its talents strained beyond the point where it can cope with the various programs discussed in the following chapter.

The Prospects of Presidential Leadership

There is no doubt that the presidency in Liberia has undergone a dramatic change during the quarter of a century of Tubman's rule. Whether he is largely a creature or a molder of events is a subject of debate among his critics and admirers. Certainly, however, for the first time in Liberian history the office of President has become a national institution rather than the peculiar plaything of the Whig minority. The ground rules of succession have been irrevocably altered, and any successor to Tubman who ignores this fundamental change in the political process does so at his peril. Whether the institution can continue to adjust to the mounting pressures from within and from without and bring off an evolutionary rather than a revolutionary transformation of the social fabric is a question that only the future historian can answer.

CHAPTER 9

To Have, but Have Not: Problems of Economic Growth

To the casual observer, Tubman's Open-Door Policy has achieved a remarkable degree of success in bringing an economically backward society so far along the road to modernization. One way of gauging progress is in terms of yearly percentage of economic growth based upon real gross national product. By this index Liberia, during the period since 1954, has found itself far ahead of its African neighbors (including Ghana, Nigeria, and the Congo) and roughly on a par with Japan, West Germany, and other developing countries.[1] The eye, moreover, confirms what the cold statistics suggest. One cannot help but be optimistic about Liberia's economic prospects when confronted with the tall office buildings rising along the Monrovia skyline, the crowded dock facilities at the Free Port and Buchanan, the feverish activity around the Bomi Hills and Nimba iron mines, the Mount Coffee hydroelectric project on the St. Paul River, the steady flow of trucks along the country's new highway network into the interior, and the variety of imported goods available in the shops of Monrovia and even in the commercial centers up-country and along the coast. The announcement in 1968 that oil deposits had been detected in the shallow waters

[1] Clower, Dalton, Harwitz, and Walters, *op. cit.*, p. 24; and *U.N. Statistical Yearbooks*, 1954–1967, *passim*.

off Monrovia gave another boost to Liberian leaders' optimism regarding the country's economic prospects.[2]

Prior to the Second World War the Republic's economy was dominated by one primary source of revenue: the rubber produced at Firestone Plantations Company. By 1967, with Liberia encouraging diversified foreign investment, there were over forty major foreign concerns and many minor ones at work in Liberia with a total investment of $750,000,000. Although the Americans still constituted the largest single group of alien investors, each year the proportion of Swedish, West German, Swiss, Israeli, Canadian, and Lebanese contributions to development has increased at the expense of the American share. By skillful manipulation of the various foreign investment groups, the Americo-Liberians have gained rather firm control of the general direction of economic growth.

The diversification of crops and other commodities has also partially liberated Liberia from the consequences of world price fluctuations for natural rubber, aggravated by competition from plastics and other substances. Citrus, bananas, coffee, and other tree crops are now cultivated on extensive plantations under concession agreements with foreign firms, and the valuable timber stands of the Liberian rain forests are now being exploited on an expanding scale. Light industries, too, contribute to the expanding revenues of the Liberian government. The public budget has dramatically exploded from a paltry $1,000,000 in 1945 to $55,887,000 in 1968.

The key to the economic miracle, however, has been iron ore. Prior to 1951, no iron ore was mined in Liberia and no one even suspected the magnitude of Liberia's nat-

[2] *West Africa,* 24 Aug. 1968, p. 986.

ural resource base. By 1967 Liberia had become not only the leading producer of iron ore in Africa, but also the third largest exporter of iron ore in the world. Beginning in 1951 with the Bomi Hills operations of the Liberian Mining Company (a subsidiary of Republic Steel), five new companies have come into production during the 1960's. Although the Mano River site of the National Iron Ore Company (consisting in large measure of Liberian stockholders) and those of DELIMCO (a German consortium) in the Bong Range are impressive, it is the operations of LAMCO (Liberian American-Swedish Minerals Company) and the Liberian Iron Ore, Ltd. (a Canadian company organized in 1966) at Nimba Mountain that have been the most impressive and have accounted for a radical transformation of the Liberian economy. It was not until 1955, when a Scottish geologist, Sandy Clark, literally stumbled on the fact that the 4,000-feet-high Nimba Mountain was practically a solid block of very high-grade iron ore that the country's growth potential was realized. Exploitation of the ore has involved the labor of several thousand workers from Liberia and neighboring states. Building a 170-mile railroad to the port facilities at Buchanan employed many more thousand laborers. New roads and the railroad have brought about the social and economic transformation of vast reaches of the country that had only nominally been under the jurisdiction of the Liberian state during the preceding century.

The Americo-Liberian elite has apparently little concern about the eventual depletion of the Nimba reserve, for the ore deposits in the Kitoma Mountain area are estimated to be comparable to those of Nimba Mountain, and the Kitoma Mining Company (an American consortium) has only commenced operations. Greater profits will come to Liberia, too, from an iron-ore washing and pelletizing plant that LAMCO opened at Buchanan in 1968. The plant permits the various grades of ore to be separated, with the immediate marketing of the high-purity pellets, which can be reduced to metallic iron faster than iron ore in its natural state.

Distress Signals

Despite the optimism regarding the iron ore production, by the mid-1960's the Liberian government found itself in the midst of a recession. To finance its expanding economy the government had borrowed heavily in the commercial money market. Its rising debt, unfortunately, coincided with a drop in world prices for both rubber and iron ore as well as with a phasing-out of the infrastructure stages of the mineral exploitation: foreign investment was reduced and workers laid off as the harbor, road, and other supporting facilities were completed. Although the government eventually weathered the crisis, it required substantial assistance from the International Monetary Fund to ease its adverse balance of payments position.

The temporary financial crisis was merely the top of the iceberg. Instead of optimism about the growth potential of Liberia, it was the conclusion of the Northwestern University economic survey team that the government should have grave concern for the economic future. According to the Northwestern group, Liberia is an extreme case of "growth without development." That is, observable economic change is not complemented by structural changes in lines of production, by adoption of more efficient techniques in the economy or government, by the significant involvement of domestic personnel in anything other than the unskilled labor category, or by new social achievements and new levels of economic aspiration. In fact, if the foreign entrepreneurs and investment were withdrawn tomorrow, the modern sector of the economy would virtually cease to function. The Northwestern team contended that the failure of true economic development is traceable ultimately to the political and social system, which leaves the tribal majority firmly under the control of the Americo-Liberian minority. Having made this indictment, the survey team suggests that "under present political and social arrangements, offering economic advice to Liberian leaders is rather futile." [3] It is against that background that we will now examine some of the more significant aspects of the Liberian economy.

Absence of Rational Planning

Among the more critical problems that have contributed to the condition criticized by the Northwestern group has been the lack of a serious and sincere commitment to planning. This can be said despite the fact that the American government, Northwestern University, Harvard University, and other experts have devoted uncounted manhours and thousands of dollars to the charade that passes for planning. Systematic record-keeping is almost an unknown art, and the need for statistical data and comprehensive surveys in carrying out development schemes has only recently become apparent to Liberian officials. Few economic priorities are established, with the result that scarce capital is dissipated on a host of projects that are

[3] The team worked in Liberia from 1961 through 1963; see Clower, Dalton, Harwitz, and Walters, *op. cit., passim.*

never completed or is squandered on prestige enterprises that add little to the basic infrastructure of a developing society. As the Northwestern group pointed out, what Liberia needs are better schools and low-cost public housing rather than first-class highways and presidential palaces; it needs not merely physical capital but improved institutional procedures and labor skills.[4]

The planning of industrial growth has been extremely chaotic. The tremendous development of rubber and iron-mining enterprises, which in 1968 accounted for over 90 per cent of Liberia's export earnings, has taken place within enclave situations: there is very little interdependence between the foreign concessions and other sectors of the economy. Few satellite industries have been created in response to the presence of the foreign concessions other than some small enterprises such as an explosives plant, a nail factory, a cement firm, an oil refinery, and an aluminum-frame window factory. Moreover, while one cannot deny the long-range value of things like palm kernel oil mills, fish canneries, shoe factories, and starch-reducing plants, some questions can be raised about the earlier priorities given to the establishment of a gin distillery, a brewery, a marble tile factory, and a television industry. Although the introduction of heavier industries may be awaiting the full utilization of the Mount Coffee hydroelectric power, to date there is little evidence that the industrialization will be carried out with the principles of development planning in mind. The latter involves, as the Northwestern team noted, "deliberate, reasoned, and orderly measures to achieve stated economic goals in determined sequence." [5]

[4] *Ibid.,* p. 94. [5] *Ibid.,* p. 77.

Transportation and Communications

Some of the more promising signs of recent economic growth are evident in the expansion of the transport network in Liberia. This not only promotes expanded production and distribution of commodities, but also facilitates political integration and control, which perhaps accounts for the high priority given this phase of economic growth. The construction of artificial harbors at Monrovia, Harper, Buchanan, and Greenville is entirely a product of the past two decades. Previously all passengers and produce brought into Liberia had to be discharged to small surfboats from ships anchored a mile or more from shore. The many rivers of Liberia have been useless for anything other than small internal trade. In the postwar period the airplane has diminished the isolation of Liberia, and Roberts International Airport is now a major field serving over twenty American, European, African, Middle East, and Latin American airlines. The airplane, however, has not alleviated the problem of internal transportation, especially where bulk commodities are concerned. The Bomi Hills, Nimba, and other iron-mining operations have led to the construction of 264 miles of railroad track by 1968. In the critical area of road construction, however, Liberia has for a long time lagged considerably behind most countries in West Africa. In 1945 there were only 206 miles of unimproved roads in the country—most of it built by Firestone—and even Monrovia lacked macadamized streets. With the help of U.S. AID loans the number of miles of all-weather roads had by 1966 increased to 2,300—with a good percentage of it either paved or laterite surfaced. The road network at long last connects Monrovia with the major settlements in the interior and knifes through large tracts of previously inaccessible forest areas. The main routes, however, are often devious, the branch road system is still primitive, and even the "all-weather" roads are frequently impassable during the torrential rains.

The Liberian communications system has lagged even further than the transportation media. Following its American model, the postal system is hopelessly tied to politics (the Postmaster-General is chairman of the True Whig Party), and it only provides service to the public in Monrovia and several of the coastal towns. A telecommunications project costing $8,500,000 was completed in 1968 but few of the long-term residents of Liberia seriously expect this to make any change in the kind of personal and official contacts maintained in the Republic.

Development of Manpower

In the absence of accurate figures on school enrollment and reliable evaluation studies of both the government and missionary efforts in this field, any assessment of the Liberian educational system is bound to be impressionistic. The consensus of most observers is that the system is at a very low stage of development, with pretension far exceeding reality. Liberia, for example, has a compulsory school attendance law; nevertheless, despite the optimistic claims of the Secretary of Education in 1967 that 120,000 children were enrolled in elementary and secondary schools, neutral observers place the estimate at a fraction of this figure—less than 10 per cent of the school-age population. Roughly one-fourth of the children, moreover, are enrolled in kindergarten and remedial first grade, and only half of the total represents survivors of the fifth grade, indicating a high dropout rate.

In many of the new states of Africa, 20 to 30 per cent of the national budget is allocated to education. By contrast the Liberian government voted only 8 per cent of its expenditures toward education during the decade from 1958 to 1968. The amount spent on schools during that period was several million dollars less than the money appropriated for the operations of the Department of State, international conferences, and the maintenance of Liberian embassies and consulates around the globe. Nor was the money for education necessarily spent wisely. Under education, the budgets contained items such as movie censorship, beauty culture, home arts, sports, and other projects of limited or even dubious educational value. A disproportionate share of the educational budget, moreover, is still allocated to foreign scholarships instead of further strengthening the sound academic facilities at Cuttington College and Our Lady of Fatima (Roman Catholic) College in Maryland, and carrying out a complete overhaul of the politics-ridden University of Liberia.[6]

At the primary and secondary school levels there are a number of qualitative and quantitative problems. Despite the obvious need for technical skills in a developing society, the emphasis of the Liberian school system is upon literacy per se or upon a classical literary education for those who advance beyond the fourth or fifth grade. There is little room in the curriculum or in practice for agricul-

[6] A. Gordon Nelson and Charles C. Hughes, "University of Liberia: An Appraisal and Recommendations with Observations and Recommendations Relative to Agriculture and Forestry" (Hectograph report, Ithaca, N.Y.: Cornell University, 1960).

ture and the mechanical arts. There are only two vocational training centers (other than those maintained by the foreign companies): the recently opened Liberian-Swedish Vocational Training Center at YeKepa in Nimba County, and the older BWI (Booker T. Washington Institute). The latter has good facilities and a qualified staff, which until 1965 was recruited by Prairie View (Texas) Agricultural and Mechanical College. BWI lacks prestige among the Americo-Liberian families, and its student body is drawn almost entirely from the ranks of tribal youngsters or lower-income Americo-Liberians. A diploma from BWI carries no political influence; it does not even guarantee one a job in a developing economy requiring mechanical and other skills. On balance, the government seems oblivious to the fact that minimal ability to read and write without the basic skills and training needed for modernization—and equally, training without opportunities to employ one's skills—is of little economic value. Indeed, it may in the long run produce only a disoriented and disaffected element in society.

There are other disturbing problems of quality in the educational system. Despite, for example, the existence of an ambitious textbook-writing program, the schools rely heavily upon ill-adapted American textbooks and upon books written by Liberian politicians. There has been, too, a lack of determination to deal realistically with the language diversity of the tribal population. Finally, it must be noted that even the officials of the Department of Education quite frankly acknowledge the generally low standards of teaching in the government-operated schools. Until 1950 over 80 per cent of primary and secondary instruction was in the hands of Christian missions. The latter received only token financial support from the government and much harassment with regard to preferential treatment of politically influential teachers and students. Although attacks on missionary efforts have been noted of late, the best testimony regarding the quality of mission education is that the nationalistic critics are the first to insist that their children be enrolled in mission schools. In the government schools patronage is highly significant in the appointment, promotion, and assignment of teachers, and the post of school supervisor is openly regarded as a convenient base for a man with political aspirations. Students at government schools are compelled to take part in a constant series of political parades and other projects unrelated to education, and they are often required to do the teachers' personal chores without pay.

One promising sign in the educational sphere has been the massive infusion of Peace Corps volunteers. Between two hundred and three hundred Peace Corps teachers each year have upgraded the quality of education in Liberia's schools, and both the Peace Corps and AID have insisted that many of the new schools be located in the neglected regions of the interior.

Reliance upon Foreign Skills and Capital

A danger point in the postwar economic scene, however, is the extent to which Americo-Liberians have relied upon foreigners in all phases of the developmental process. Admittedly, a massive infusion of external capital has been required to get development under way. Americo-Liberians are quick to point out that their country did not have the "advantages" of the British Colonial Welfare and Development Act or the comparable French schemes, which stimulated postwar economic development in other African states. Nevertheless, the wealthier and better-educated Americo-Liberians could invest both their talents and their money to a considerably greater extent in the development of their own country. Few are interested in the launching and practical management of new economic enterprises. Although they may be prepared to underwrite foreign management, they are reluctant to lend funds to small Liberian businessmen. Similarly, despite much talk about cooperative societies and a development loan corporation for small businessmen, the Liberian government has not chosen to disperse its patronage among small Liberian businessmen.[7] Furthermore, neither have the major concessionaires felt obliged to train Liberians for management or skilled technical posts in their enterprises as long as the government continues its practice of hiring away the better-trained personnel at the end of the training course. In the long run the failure of the government to insist upon a Liberianization of the economy may react to the detriment of the Americo-Liberian ruling class and the foreign economic interests. It is difficult to see how the country can be forever insulated against a violent nationalist reaction to this situation by both the tribal element and the lower ranks of the Americo-Liberian community.

Liberian control over the concessionaires has been noticeably firmer in recent years. Each renewal of an agreement, for example, sets up more stringent regulations regarding the exact areas for exploitation, the type of production allowed, the conditions of labor, the extent of taxation, and other details. The government also has insisted upon ownership of a considerable fraction of the

[7] Mitchell, *op. cit.,* p. 51.

company shares and extra provisions regarding scholarships, positions on the board of directors for Liberians, and other benefits. Needless to say, the benefits are often monopolized by the Americo-Liberian ruling group, and very little trickles down to the masses. For their part, the concessionaires have raised their demands by insisting that labor union activity be curtailed or that workers' compensation legislation not be enforced. Firestone, whether inadvertently or by design, has insured itself against future nationalization by distributing free rubber seedlings to the "honorables." The processing of the rubber still remains a Firestone enterprise, however, and thus a strong economic coalition has been formed.

A similar posture has been clearly developing during recent years with respect to the Lebanese. Except for some very small shopkeepers and the Mandingo traders ("Charlies"), the commercial activities of Monrovia and other urban centers are dependent upon the Lebanese. As indicated above, their presence serves as a safety valve against revolutionary change. Yet each year the price of Lebanese existence in Liberia rises as new devices are erected to redirect some of the profits into government revenues or the pockets of officials. One of the latest measures was enacted in 1968. This requires all shopkeepers in the country to deposit $10,000 in Monrovia banks as "caution money" to cover any commercial dishonesty. It was reported that twenty shops had closed within the first three months of 1968. Undoubtedly the bulk of the Lebanese will remain, and the higher cost of operation will be passed on to the tribal and lower-class Americo-Liberian consumer.

One very significant way that Liberia capitalizes upon foreign enterprise without a significant investment of Liberian entrepreneurial skill is the registration of foreign ships under the Liberian "flag of convenience." In serving as an "international Delaware," the West African republic ranked among the seven largest maritime powers during the decade from 1956 to 1966. In 1967, Liberia actually forged to the head of the list, ahead of the U.S., Britain, Norway, Japan, the U.S.S.R., and Greece. The Liberian government secures a considerable revenue in this fashion from American and European shipowners, who take advantage of Liberia's lax laws on employment, safety, and fees. In 1964, Liberia became more directly involved when two Liberian-owned companies purchased ships that—at least in theory—were manned by Liberians.

Agricultural Bias of the Population

Despite dramatic strides in the exploitation of Liberia's mineral resources and the emergence of urban clusters, between 80 and 90 per cent of the population still live in the rural areas. Some cultivate rice, cassava, plantain, and other staples. An increasing number are involved in the production, processing, and marketing of tree crops for export. Rubber has dominated and seems to be on the increase despite its uneasy position in the materials market. Indeed, in 1966 the U.S. Rubber Company provided additional competition to Firestone and Goodrich, which have been producing in Liberia for a number of years. Tubman, moreover, in 1964 gently suggested that Firestone was "duty bound" to plant rubber in the entire million acres of land that had been leased to it. Although rubber remains the largest single export crop, attempts have been made to diversify the cash-crop economy through the expansion of coffee, cocoa, palm kernel, citrus fruit, piassava, and kola nut production.

Most Liberian tree crops are grown on plantations rather than on small farms. Of the rubber processed by Firestone Plantations, for example, roughly 80 per cent is grown on its own estates, with the remainder being grown on the farms of the more than one thousand members of the Independent Rubber Planters Association. A few politician absentee-owners account for a high percentage of the association's crop. In general, efforts to encourage tribal Liberians to grow tree crops or other cash commodities are only slowly yielding results. Liberia, indeed, finds itself today in the embarrassing position of having to import rice, the staple of the Liberian diet, despite the fact that its population is primarily committed to agricultural production. Operation Production was launched by the President in 1964 not only to help correct that situation but also to further diversify and increase agricultural production throughout the country. Tubman noted in his 1968 Inaugural Address that the program had failed to achieve many of its goals. Indeed, it seemed to have succeeded largely to the extent that coercive measures have been used. Urban vagrants in Monrovia, for example, have been rounded up and sent back to the hinterland to farm. The chiefs, too, have been warned by the President that if they failed to meet their quotas of increased production in rice and other commodities, they would be fined $2,000 each; if this did not bring the desired results, the chiefs would be replaced. Needless to say, the most significant force has been the chastized chiefs' pressure on the peasants. The response of the tribal people to all this is aptly summed up by the Northwestern volume, which suggests that "even the most eloquent advocate of economic progress cannot demonstrate the advantage of growing two grains of rice where only one flourished before if the prospective grower knows that both grains will go to someone else." [8]

The tribal people are still overwhelmingly wedded to a subsistence economy. There have, of course, been exceptions. Long before the Americo-Liberians arrived, some of the hinterland tribes had established market centers in which various types of crude currency were employed. There existed also a rather sophisticated form of inter-tribal production and exchange of arts and crafts. During the past three decades individual tribesmen have been brought into the cash economy in increasing numbers as wage-earners on large estates or at the mines, as partici-pants in tribal communal enterprises, or even as small farmers. Typically, however, the food that the tribal family consumes is the food that the family collectively produces. Little is left over for exchange. Family plots are small and must be numerous to accommodate the fallow system of rotation and the slash-and-burn technique of bringing new land under the hoe. Farms are normally held under usufructuary right of occupancy, with only a small per-centage of the tribal people of the hinterland attempting to acquire private leaseholds. The threat that Americo-Liberian land hunger poses to future stability is discussed at length in Chapter 11.

Absence of Distributive Justice

Perhaps the most critical problem in Liberia's economic growth is the absence of distributive justice. While ex-ploitation of the tremendous natural resources has brought

[8] Clower, Dalton, Harwitz, and Walters, *op. cit.,* p. 33.

wealth to the country and has managed to affect the lives
of all except those in the remotest reaches of the interior,
the benefits are dispersed in a highly inequitable fashion.
The Northwestern team estimated that the 97 per cent of
the population classified as tribal or lower-class Americo-
Liberian received only 25 per cent of the share of national
income, and "this share is not likely to expand in the years
to come unless deliberate action is taken to alter both the
structure of the economy and the distribution of aggregate
earnings." [9] The remaining 75 per cent of the national income was distributed to the foreign households and business firms and to the 3 per cent of the Liberian population
that constitutes the political elite.

Seeking an analogy for the dramatic economic growth
that benefits only the ruling elite, the Northwestern team
concluded that it "was as though a country club has suddenly expanded its revenues." [10] In contrast to the general
poverty of the tribal masses, the standard of living of the
"honorable" class has been immeasurably altered as a consequence of the rapid growth of the economy and the
government subsidization of the Whig class discussed in
Chapter 7. In itself, Liberia's system of preferential treatment and graft does not differ radically from that of other
countries of the world. What makes the Liberian case so
critical is that the benefits accrue to a very close-knit minority while the wages for the tribal people involved in the
highly inflated money economy seldom exceed fifty cents a
day. Moreover, efforts of the tribal people to enhance their
bargaining position through cooperatives and trade unions
have been crassly discouraged. Indeed, the most striking
result of the dramatic change in the Liberian economy is

[9] *Ibid.,* p. 67.   [10] *Ibid.,* p. 95.

that the new roads make it easier for the Americo-Liberians—officials and nonofficials alike—to exploit the tribal hinterland through labor recruitment, the imposition of extraordinary taxes, and the constant requisitioning of crops and livestock. One can readily agree that "roads that bring good government to backward areas are clearly a blessing; roads that bring bad government may be a curse." [11]

[11] *Ibid.,* p. 33.

CHAPTER 10

A Place in the Sun:
Liberia in World Affairs

Liberia's relations with the outside world have not always been of its own choosing. Cast adrift on alien shores, the Americo-Liberian settlers were compelled as a matter of survival to devise effective means for neutralizing their relatively hostile environment. Immediately behind the coastal settlements were the Vai, Grebo, Kru, and others with whom they came into constant conflict over questions of land, trade, and cultural identity. Their other adversaries—the British and French colonialists, operating out of bases in Sierra Leone, the Ivory Coast, and Guinea —challenged the extended claims of the settlers not only to the interior but to the coastal areas as well. Occasionally, too, the Americo-Liberians found their suzerainty challenged by freebooting slave traders, such as Pedro Blanco, who incited the tribal people to rebellion whenever the settlers made inroads into the slave-raiding areas of the Europeans and Brazilians. An effective foreign policy then was vital for the survival of the settlers and their descendants against a variety of threats.

Liberian-American Relations

Considering the history of Liberian settlement, it was perhaps inevitable that the Republic's external orientation during much of its history should be stronger toward the

United States than toward any other state or dependency.
Even during the nineteenth century, when the long-
delayed official recognition of Liberia was followed by only
token or moral support to the settlers in their disputes
with Britain and France, the American connections were
firmly maintained through nonofficial channels. Not only
did the activities of Protestant missionaries provide organizational and personal ties between Americans and the
colonists, but they were also responsible for most of the
educational and health programs in the country. On a very
personal level, too, the family ties that spanned the ocean
remained strong and actually increased as Liberian students and visitors to the United States acquired American
spouses.

The twentieth century witnessed the expansion of a
variety of nongovernmental connections. Firestone Plantations Company, for example, pioneered the economic development of the country, and it has been followed of late
by a host of other American investors and commercial
firms. American universities, too, have been involved in
the development of Liberia. Only the Nigerians account
for a higher percentage of the African students in the
United States. Cornell University, Prairie View (Texas)
Agricultural and Mechanical College, Northwestern University, and Harvard University have been even more directly involved by providing assistance to the Liberian government and to educational institutions in the country.
Other private institutions, such as the Rockefeller Foundation and the Eli Lilly Foundation, have been actively
combating the problems of disease, illiteracy, and economic underdevelopment.

At the official level as well, the contacts between the two

republics have expanded during recent years. The military assistance the United States gave Liberia in 1915 to quell an uprising on the Kru Coast was continued in a more-or-less sporadic manner until the period following World War II. Now the training and the equipping of Liberian troops by the United States have been put on a permanent basis. In 1959, Liberia became the first—and thus far the only—African state to conclude a mutual defense pact with the United States. In terms of economic assistance, too, Liberia has been the prime African beneficiary of lend-lease aid, technical assistance programs, and loans from the Export-Import Bank and AID (Agency for International Development). The independence of Nigeria and other new African states was expected to diminish Liberia's role in African-American relations. Relatively speaking, this has happened, but in absolute terms the American interest in Liberia has continued to expand at a significant rate (see Table 4). In addition to emergency measures, such as the sale of rice in 1966 at low cost under the Food for Peace Program, the United States has provided technical assistance in the fields of road construction, agriculture, forestry, veterinary science, fish production, public administration, and mapping and geodetic survey. The greatest technical assistance, however, has been in the field of education, and especially since the Peace Corps in 1962 began sending more than two hundred new volunteers to Liberia each year on two-year contracts.

AID has been one of the most significant continuing sources for needed investment funds. Either through direct loans or guarantees of private investment, the United States has been instrumental during the 1961–1968 period in securing a $5,300,000 modern teaching hospital for

Monrovia, several hundred school buildings at the coast and in the interior, a $27,000,000 hydroelectric plant on the St. Paul River, a $7,200,000 expansion of the capital's sanitation system, and major improvements in Liberia's over-all transportation and communication network.

Table 4. U.S. economic assistance to Liberia, fiscal years 1946–1968 (in millions of dollars)

	pre-1962	1962	1963	1964	1965	1966	1967	1968	1946–1968
AID and predecessor agencies									
Loan	3.1	—	28.4	7.4	9.3	1.4	1.8	4.7	56.1
Grant	26.2	10.6	7.8	6.5	6.7	6.6	5.5	5.3	75.2
Total	29.3	10.6	36.2	13.9	16.0	8.0	7.3	10.0	131.3
Food for Peace	1.0	.8	.9	1.1	.2	1.1	.4	1.1	6.6
Export–Import bank loans	79.4	—	—	—	23.1	—	—	—	102.5
Other (incl. Peace Corps)	7.9	.5	1.6	2.2	2.8	2.6	2.8	2.8	23.2
Total economic assistance	117.6	11.9	38.7	17.2	42.1	11.7	10.5	13.9	263.6

From USAID, *Contact,* I (July–Sept., 1968), p. 8.

Liberian officials have been rather ambivalent about the relationship of their country to the United States. On the one hand, they feel that American aid has been too small in relation to need and has "too many strings attached." There is undoubtedly a sincere conviction in the constant repetition of the theme that the United States has a debt to Liberia stemming from its origins as a quasi-American colony and from the injustices that the ancestors of the Americo-Liberians suffered at the hands of Southern slave-owners. A more recent debt has been incurred as a result of Liberia's following the lead of the United States in entering both world wars against the Germans. In World War II, Liberia provided the Allied forces with land for an important military base, was the major source of natural rubber following the fall of Malaya, and made many sacrifices it need not have made had the country remained neutral. Most recently Liberia has given the United States a considerable advantage in the Cold War by permitting the construction of a Voice of America transmitter powerful enough to cover the entire African continent. During Tubman's visit to Washington in March, 1968, he indicated support for the American position in Viet Nam.

At the same time as they stress this theme of American responsibility for Liberia, Liberian officials are concerned about the intensification of relations with the United States. Sensitive to the charge of African and European leaders that Liberia is the "slave and enclave of the dollar," the Liberian government has been attempting to diversify the sources of its foreign investment and to establish a complex of bilateral and multilateral agreements with countries in all quarters of the globe. Liberia now has embassies in most countries of Western Europe, Africa, and the Near East as well as Haiti and Taiwan. Despite the lack of formal diplomatic relations, Liberian officials have established contacts with or have visited the Soviet Union, Eastern Europe, and Communist China. Liberia is using the facilities of the United Nations to the fullest extent possible to emphasize its independence of action in foreign affairs, and on several occasions the Liberians have found themselves taking an opposing view to that of the United States.

Relations with Europe and Asia

Although the American shield has been useful in guaranteeing Liberia's survival in the past, Liberian leaders in the period since World War II have appreciated that control over their own affairs could only be secured through an intensification of their contacts with other parts of the world. Membership in the United Nations, of which Liberia is a charter member, has given it an obvious channel for this purpose, but it was not until other states in Africa achieved independence that she began the full utilization of this forum. Liberia increasingly finds it more profitable in terms of securing economic and political goals to engage in a series of bilateral arrangements with European and Asian states. Although the American presence has remained strong, each year the proportion of American involvement in the Liberian economy has diminished as governmental aid and private investment from European and Asian sources has increased. In trade, for example, figures available in 1968 indicated that the American share of Liberia's exports dropped from 90 per cent in 1950 to 46 per cent in 1965, while Liberia's imports from the United States dropped from 71 to 47 per cent of the total. An increasing share of the trade relations each year is assumed by West Germany, Britain, Japan, Sweden, the Netherlands, and Italy.

A further index of the rising European and Asian presence versus American involvement in Liberia is revealed in the census figures for 1962. Roughly a third of the aliens came from other African states. Of the remaining aliens, the American presence was still considerable—1,645 out of 21,365 (8 per cent). They were outranked, however, by the Lebanese with 2,077 residents (10 per cent) and by the collective representation from Western Europe (15 per cent). The Europeans came from the following countries: Italy, 699; Netherlands, 481; Spain, 470; Sweden, 383; United Kingdom, 293; West Germany, 275; France, 210; Switzerland, 125; Denmark, 47; Norway, 28; Belgium, 24; Undesignated, 198. Each of the foreign groups tends to make a distinct contribution. The Lebanese, for example, are engaged largely in the merchandising of commodities throughout the country; most of the Italians are building roads; the Swedes and West Germans are concentrated around the mining enterprises at Nimba and the Bong Hills; the Dutch usually handle the major external trading operations; and the Swiss, for the most part, are involved in managerial positions in commercial firms or at the major rubber plantations.

The Open-Door Policy has thus recruited the required alien personnel for the sustained growth of the Liberian economy, and in the process has kept to a minimum a Liberian entrepreneurial class that could challenge the present political regime. The expansion of Liberia's external commitments, moreover, has brought in foreign governmental aid, the diversification of its trading relationships, increased technical assistance, more scholarships for Liberian students, and private investment. There is little doubt, too, that the Liberian leadership has banked upon its new international agreements, reaffirmed by rather frequent exchanges of official visits, to shore up its world prestige. Like Israel, Liberia today feels that it must have friends to defend its interests in a world it still regards as relatively hostile. Although it has avoided strong ties with the Communist bloc, it has forged significant links with many of the neutralist states such as Austria, Switzerland, India, and the Scandinavian group or with countries that are not always popular with Liberia's more nationalistic and socialistic friends in Africa. Included in this list are Belgium, Nationalist China, Spain, and Haiti. There is also the strong relationship that Liberia—along with several of its African neighbors—has established with Israel.

Intra-African Relations

It has been noted previously that Liberian leaders viewed the impending liberation of Liberia's African neighbors with some trepidation, for it opened both new and potentially hostile frontiers. Despite the intensification of intra-African contacts during the Second World War and its aftermath, Liberia found itself largely isolated from continental affairs on the eve of Ghana's independence in 1957. The continued heavy reliance of Liberia upon American support was only one of the factors contributing to this isolation. Geography was another, for the rough terrain made it difficult for the Liberians to build roads and bridges connecting Monrovia with its own hinterland let alone reaching the French and British territories beyond. European politics was also a factor, inasmuch as Liberia was excluded from the British and French colonial systems, which at least had led to some interterritorial cooperation between Nigeria and Sierra Leone, on the one hand, and Senegal and the Ivory Coast, on the other. The critical attitudes Europeans assumed with respect to the ability of the Americo-Liberians to govern themselves were frequently adopted by African leaders as well.[1] Isolation, however, was also a product of choice by

[1] Nnamdi Azikiwe's *Liberia in World Politics* (London: Stockwell, 1934), a more contemporary indictment, echoes the criticisms expressed by Dr. Edward Wilmot Blyden.

the Americo-Liberians, who rejected their African heritage in favor of an emphasis upon their Western background.

Such contact as did take place between Liberians and other West Africans was largely personal in character. Family ties, for example, between the Creoles of Sierra Leone and the Americo-Liberians remained strong, as did those among the tribal peoples separated by the arbitrarily drawn international boundaries. The parents of Americo-Liberian youths in many cases recognized the superior standard of schools in the Gold Coast and Sierra Leone and sent them there for education. Better employment opportunities lured the Kru people as well as many Americo-Liberians to Nigeria and Senegal.

The achievement of independence by Ghana in 1957 and Guinea in 1958 had a profound impact upon Liberia. Not only was the Republic permitted for the first time to establish direct official relations with other West African governments, but such ties were recognized as vital for survival. The rising wave of African nationalism posed a threat both to the supremacy of the settler community within the Republic and to Liberia's claim to a major share of the technical and other forms of assistance given through the United Nations to developing countries in Africa. This is a plausible explanation for the almost frenzied efforts of the Liberian government to establish ties with the new states and to assume a role of leadership in the United Nations and at the various conferences of African states. Despite the considerable drain upon its financial resources (roughly one-tenth of the national budget) and upon its pool of educated talent Liberia has established embassies in each of the new African countries. Exchanges of visits between Tubman and other African heads of state are frequent and often lead to the signing of bilateral agreements on trade, cultural exchanges, and other matters. Liberian officials each year attend an average of fifty conferences on African problems or the general condition of developing societies.

In the decade since 1957, Liberia has served as the host country for many major African conferences. Perhaps the most significant of these was the largely unheralded meeting in the remote interior at Sanniquellie in 1959. It was there that Nkrumah's plans for a political union of African states suffered a severe setback. The most famous of the Liberian international gatherings, however, took place in Monrovia in May, 1961. At that conference the cleavage deepened between the more revolutionary states of Africa (the Casablanca bloc) and the moderate or conservative powers (the Monrovia group).

Liberia's claim to speak for other African states in the United Nations was given symbolic recognition in December, 1960, by its selection as the first African state to be seated on the Security Council. In the various organs of the United Nations the Liberian delegates have seized the mantle of leadership within the African caucus, mounting a steady campaign of criticism against South Africa for its policy of *apartheid* and its administration of Southwest Africa, against Portugal for its repression of African nationalism in Angola and Mozambique, and against Britain for not having taken a more vigorous stand in Rhodesia. Why Liberia has been allowed to assume the leadership is a mystery to many, given the previous hostility of Nigerian, Ghanaian and other African elites. In part it may have been purely practical considerations: Liberia, among all the states in Africa, appeared to have the financial means and the educated personnel to spare for the diplomatic advancement of African causes. Its special relationship with the United States—obviously a distinct disadvantage in many instances—did give Liberia diplomatic and other forms of access to the most powerful member of the international community. Finally, deference to Tubman's seniority spared many African leaders from having to recognize the self-acclaimed leadership of Kwame Nkrumah. This was particularly important to the leaders of Nigeria, Sierra Leone, and most of the French-speaking states, who regarded Nkrumah's international role as a threat to domestic stability within their own countries.

Whether or not its leadership was appreciated by other African states, Liberia's leaders felt that the new posture was vital for survival. Unless it magnified its importance in intra-African affairs, even its special relationship with the United States was likely to be diminished, with more and more foreign aid directed to Nigeria, Ghana, and other larger and more activist states. Unless Liberia took positive stands on issues, African leadership would be monopolized by the radical group at the opposite ideological pole from Liberia. This explains why Liberia during the Congo crisis provided troops for the United Nations efforts and involved itself diplomatically in the undermining of Lumumba and Gizenga. It accounts, too, for the rather ubiquitous presence of Liberians in most of the United Nations specialized agencies. Liberia uses its membership in the World Health Organization, UNESCO, and other bodies not only to expand its own channels for technical assistance but to advance more general African causes as well. With the exception of the ILO, where it is occasionally attacked for its labor practices, the Liberians in the United Nations have been highly successful in their attempt to capture the role of spokesman for Africa.

Liberia's relations with the more conservative and pro-Western African states are generally more cordial than with those countries that tend to take more radical positions on world problems, relations with the West, Pan-Africanism, and development of Socialist economies. Tubman, for example, has gone out of his way to establish very special links with Emperor Haile Selassie I of Ethiopia, President Habib Bourguiba of Tunisia, the leaders of many French-speaking states of West and Central Africa, and even with Malawi's President, Hastings Kamuzu Banda, who has committed the cardinal sin in the eyes of many by establishing relations with South Africa. Tubman has also taken relatively bold and unpopular stances in defense of Moise Tshombe, both during his leadership of the Congo in 1964 and during his detention in Algeria in 1967. On the other hand, his relations with Ghana during the Nkrumah period and with Mali, Algeria, and the United Arab Republic have ranged from studied correctness to outright hostility. At various points in the past Tubman has expelled Nkrumah's and Nasser's diplomatic personnel for alleged interference in Liberian internal affairs.

Of particular concern to the Tubman regime has been the relationship between Liberia and its more immediate neighbors. Potentially, Sierra Leone might have constituted a threat to the Americo-Liberians, for the state, even before its independence in 1961, had come under the control of the tribal people of the hinterland. Despite the overlapping tribal ties of the Mende, Gola, Kissi, and others and the links between the Americo-Liberians and their Sierra Leone counterparts, the Creoles, relations be-

tween the two governments have remained cordial. The
military regime that took over in Sierra Leone in 1967 appeared to be as conservative as the preceding governments
of Sir Milton and Sir Albert Margai. The ascendancy of
the more liberal Siaka Stevens, however, caused some concern in Monrovia. The only major source of irritation
between the two states, however, appears to be the substantial revenue loss that Sierra Leone sustains as a result
of diamond smuggling. Many of the diamonds that enter
the world market through Monrovia apparently have been
mined in the Kono district of Sierra Leone. Liberia's eastern neighbor, the Ivory Coast, has also generally maintained good relations with the Tubman government, inasmuch as Premier Félix Houphouët-Boigny shares Tubman's views on Pan-Africanism, capitalism, and relations
with the West. One issue dividing the two countries has
been the Ivory Coast's attempt to market its coffee in the
U.S. Moreover, the continuing hostility between the Ivory
Coast and their mutual neighbor, Guinea, has raised the
spectre of disorder on Liberia's borders. Tubman has tried
to play the role of mediator in reducing the level of ten-
sion between the two hostile states.

The greatest concern has been Guinea. As the successors
to the French, the Guineans inherited the series of boundary disputes with Liberia, especially those relating to the
ownership of the iron-rich Nimba Mountain. The more
threatening problem, however, has been the ideological
chasm separating the True Whig Party and Sékou Touré's
Parti Démocratique de Guinée. The latter, in seeking the
rapid political, social, and economic mobilization of all
elements within society along socialist lines, has stood in
sharp contrast to the True Whig Party. As a result, more-

over, of the ruthless fashion in which de Gaulle withdrew from Guinea at the time of independence, Sékou Touré was forced to search for other friends in order to stave off economic collapse. The Soviet bloc eagerly stepped into this void. Thus, the major protagonists of the Cold War found their respective major spheres of influence in Africa face to face at the Guinean-Liberian border.

Nonetheless, Sékou Touré and William Tubman have arrived at a harmonious *modus vivendi*. Strangely enough —given the difference in age, background, ideological orientation, and other factors—a rather remarkable friendship has developed between these two West African leaders during the past decade. One of the significant considerations has been the dependence of Guinea upon the Liberian roads and the Free Port of Monrovia in getting its goods from eastern Guinea into the world market. The longer route to Conakry as well as the general shortage of fuel in Guinea has made the Liberian route to the sea vital. Moreover, the agreement permitting Guinea to use the new railroad from Nimba to the port of Buchanan has made it economically feasible for Guinea to mine the iron ore found in its portion of the Nimba Range. Hence, there are sound reasons for Sékou Touré's implicit self-restraint in exporting revolution to Liberia. There are few restrictions on the movement of Liberian and Guinean nationals across their frontiers for social or economic contact.

Pan-Africanism

Perhaps the oddest element in the Tubman-Touré friendship has been the acceptance by the Guinean President of Tubman's viewpoint on Pan-Africanism, despite Touré's earlier collaboration with Nkrumah. Indeed, in a sense, Tubman and Touré were thrown together by Nkrumah.[2] It is true that Nkrumah's electrifying announcement in November, 1958, that Ghana and Guinea had united provided Touré with the kind of psychological boost he needed at that moment both at home and abroad. Gradually, however, Touré found Nkrumah's embrace somewhat suffocating. Tubman, for his part, found the prospect of Nkrumah as his next-door neighbor a direct challenge to the Liberian political system. In opposition to the Nkrumah posture that Pan-African unity had to be achieved immediately, politically, and on a continental plane, Tubman gradually evolved a counterversion of Pan-Africanism that emphasized gradualism, economic and cultural cooperation as a precursor to political discussion, and regional rather than continental cooperation.

Tubman's diplomatic victory in his discussions with Nkrumah and Touré at Sanniquellie in 1959, I regard as one of the landmarks in the history of the Pan-African movement. Tubman effectively undermined the Nkrumah approach and in the process loosened the bonds between Touré and the Ghanaian leader. Indeed, by the time of Nkrumah's overthrow in 1966, the political experiment represented by the expanded Guinea-Ghana-Mali union was in ashes, and Guinea found itself in a regional customs union that linked it with three of the more conservative states of West Africa: Sierra Leone, the Ivory Coast, and Liberia. Although the Organization for West African Economic Cooperation has not functioned as effectively as its

[2] For a fuller discussion of this problem, see my article, "Which Road to Pan-African Unity? The Sanniquellie Conference, 1959," in Gwendolen M. Carter, ed. *Politics in Africa* (New York: Harcourt, Brace and World, 1966), pp. 1–32.

advocates hoped it would, its creation was important. It demonstrated once again the manner in which Tubman has been able to use his remarkable talents in international diplomacy to reduce a clear and present ideological threat to Liberia's domestic stability.

At the continental level as well, Liberia's posture on Pan-African cooperation was welcomed by many African leaders who viewed Nkrumah's activities as unrealistic, if not threatening. The Monrovia Conference of May, 1961; the Lagos Conference of 1962; and the Addis Ababa Conference of May, 1963, represented victories for the Tubman point of view on Pan-Africanism. The Charter of the Organization of African Unity adopted at Addis Ababa was watermarked "Made in Liberia." In its functioning since 1963, the OAU has failed to be the dynamic force in African affairs which Nkrumah had hoped, and Tubman had feared, it might be.

Summary

During the Tubman period Liberia has managed to execute almost a complete reversal of its relatively isolationist stance. Without abandoning its ties with America—even increasing them in terms of economic, cultural, and military assistance—it has forged an independent, activist role in international politics. New links with Asia and Europe have given it more maneuverability in resisting demands from the United States. Its new ties with its African neighbors have reduced the dangers of ideological threats closer to home. From a position of low repute in the attitudes of African elites elsewhere on the continent, it has been permitted to claim the mantle of leadership in pressing African causes. Thus, it has managed to neutralize the potentially hostile environment in which it finds itself by pursuing an activist foreign policy. In a curious way, too, the activist foreign policy provides yet another hedge against revolution by providing an outlet for the pool of young educated talent that is intentionally thwarted in the economic transformation of Liberia.

CHAPTER 11

A "Bright" Tomorrow?

The quarter of a century during which Tubman has ruled Liberia has provided the Americo-Liberians with new and more effective techniques for the art of political survival. In many respects the twentieth-century threats posed to the Whig autocracy by African nationalism in neighboring states have constituted even greater challenges than the hostility of the physical environment, tribal resistance, and the machinations of the European colonial powers that had to be overcome by the founding settlers in the nineteenth century. Although Liberia as a whole has undoubtedly gained, it was the decidedly good fortune of the Americo-Liberian class that the modern challenge to its supremacy found its hero. Tubman— frequently over the strenuous opposition of those whose interests have prospered—has displayed a talent for political imagination and manipulation far exceeding any of his predecessors.

Tubman's Open-Door Policy, for example, has ingeniously expanded the financial means for continued subsidizing of the system of Americo-Liberian privilege. At the same time, the revenues from iron ore, rubber, and other resources have provided the financial and technical means for the suppression, seduction, and control of dissent on the part of the tribal majority. The foreigner in the nineteenth century was considered an overt threat to Americo-Liberian supremacy in the tribal hinterland; in the present era the foreigner has become the witting or unwitting partner in the exploitation of the tribal masses. President Tubman's foreign policy programs, moreover, have skillfully injected Liberia into world affairs and ended Liberia's isolation from its African neighbors. As a consequence, Tubman has managed to neutralize the potential hostility of his neighboring African leaders, who have committed themselves to a different kind of political, social, and economic revolution for the people of their countries. Finally, Tubman's extension of suffrage and representation to the tribal hinterland and the implementation of his Unification Program have provided at least the semblance of greater access for the tribal people to the citadels of political, social, and economic power in Liberia.

The key to the continued success of Tubman's evolutionary approach to change lies largely in the future of the Unification Program. There is abundant evidence that in official circumstances at least, the many historic barriers to legal, political, and social equality between the tribal masses and the descendants of the founding settlers are being eroded. Public arrogance on the part of Americo-Liberians toward tribal people—still blatant during the administration of Edwin Barclay—is becoming rarer, and the flagrant abuse of basic substantive and procedural rights has been largely curbed during the Tubman era. In more positive terms, the Unification Program has encouraged the tribal people to take a measure of pride in their antecedents, their art and language, and even their traditional names. Foreign and Liberian scholars are being invited to portray more accurately the tribal contribution to the making of modern Liberia. Finally, the tribal people have at last come to realize that the President of Liberia is also their President. As a popular political figure who has evidenced warmth, humor, and the ability to render substantive justice, Tubman has done much to bridge the gap separating the two communities in Liberia.

The Limits of Unification

The cultural integration of the settler and tribal communities is, however, far from complete. Although public abuse has diminished, covert discrimination in governmental service as well as in social relationships continues. Tribal people still tend to regard themselves as Bassa, Kpelle, or Loma, reserving the title "Liberian" for the Americo-Liberians. While the law is purposely vague on the point, it is apparent that a legal distinction has been perpetuated between the two communities in matters of marriage and divorce, jurisdiction of tribal and statutory courts, and the occupation of land in the interior. Oddly enough, when legal distinctions have been eliminated, the situation usually works to the monetary and political advantage of the corps of Americo-Liberian lawyers and their young tribal proteges and to the decided disadvantage of the illiterate tribal peasant, who finds himself trapped in the unfamiliar procedures of the Liberian court system which is now spreading throughout the hinterland counties.[1] Frequently, moreover, the Westernized tribal youth finds himself in the frustrating position of having his claim to "civilized" status rejected both by his tribal kin and by the Americo-Liberian elite. There are still serious obstacles to the easy acquisition of the certificate that exempts a

[1] Jerry L. Prillaman, "Integration of Tribal Courts into the National Judiciary of Liberia: the Role of the Local Courts Advisor," *Liberian Law Journal*, II (June 1966), pp. 43–67.

tribal person from compulsory labor, porter service, and the jurisdiction of tribal courts. Thus, his kinsmen continue to hold him responsible for the traditional obligations with respect to his family and to tribal political leaders despite his superior education, his acceptance of Christianity, and his involvement in the money economy.

Although in relative terms the material lot of the tribal people has been substantially improved by the rapid economic exploitation of Liberia's resources, in absolute terms the gains of the tribal people are small when contrasted with those of the Americo-Liberian elite. Each year the gap between the extremes of income becomes greater, while the restraints upon training opportunities and the upward mobility of tribal people in the economy are eased only slightly. Moreover, only the rigorous and persistent prodding of American and other foreign advisers has persuaded the government to take into account the urgent needs of the tribal areas for new schools or hospitals, government scholarships, and welfare programs. Although the Peace Corps effort in particular has led to some correction of the gross imbalances, much still remains to be done.

In the long run the greatest economic irritant may still be the initial source of antagonism between the founding settlers and the indigenous tribal leaders: land. Quietly but steadily, as the new roads have penetrated the hinterland, the "honorables" and others who have the ear of the President have engaged in one of the most extensive programs of private land acquisition outside of South Africa, Rhodesia, and the Portuguese dependencies. The actual extent of the transfer of title from tribal land to freehold land is not a matter of public record, for only the less consequential registrations of title are published in the press.

So outrageous has the covert acquisition of land been that President Tubman himself in his Inaugural Address of 1964 commented on the situation. He noted that several citizens—including the chiefs allied with the Americo-Liberian ruling class—had acquired estates of up to twenty thousand acres, for as little as fifty cents an acre. "One day," Tubman warned, "the growing educated population in the rural areas might find themselves without land, which would have been bought up by Monrovia folk." [2] It is the President's office, incidentally, which authorizes the transfer of titles, and the President's own holdings are substantial.

Self-Interest, Group Interest, and Political Stability

The question of whether the evolutionary pace of change that leaves the Americo-Liberian ruling class firmly in control will give way to a more revolutionary approach that promises a more egalitarian society depends ultimately upon the attitudes and actions of the young generation of Liberians, both Americo-Liberian and tribal.

One of the striking features of Liberia today is that few of the beneficiaries of the system of privilege enter the jobs that are most critical to the continuation of Whig control. For example, the role of district commissioner in the hinterland areas has become a position of increasingly strategic proportions. New roads, the growth of trading centers inland, the fluid migration of tribal people, and new economic enterprises call for more rigorous surveillance. But being posted to the hinterland as a district commissioner—far from the bright lights and the vital center of politics in Monrovia—has little appeal to the

[2] *West Africa,* 1 Feb. 1964, p. 120.

sons of the more prominent Americo-Liberian families. By default, then, the job goes to an individual who has perhaps only a rudimentary education and comes from a family whose origins are either lower-class Americo-Liberian or even tribal (assuming that his loyalty to the regime has been demonstrated). The consequence is that the district commissioner is not particularly committed to the perpetuation of a system that gives greater favors and rewards to the urban aristocracy at the coast. To the lower-class Americo-Liberian from Monrovia, the remote interior district takes on all the attributes of a "punishment station." He attempts to compensate for his low political status and overcome his sense of personal frustration. He tends, for example, to engage in extensive purchasing of land (despite the specific legal provision against such conflict of interest), to use local labor for his farm, and to perform other acts that advance his own personal interests but further antagonize the tribal masses toward the system of government he represents. Indeed, lacking the kind of family connections that sustain the Americo-Liberian official through good fortunes and bad, the lower-status district commissioner feels compelled to make the best of his opportunities while he can.

If anything, this situation seems to have been magnified by the 1964 extension of the county system to the former provinces. A whole new layer of jobs was created. Although some of the senatorial and house seats were assumed by bona fide members of the Whig aristocracy, the rest went to Western-educated tribal persons, as did many of the new administrative and legal posts in the new system. Thus, the bright tribal person who had demonstrated his loyalty to the regime has been given the chance of actively involving himself in local politics, foregoing for the time being his ambitions to participate at the national level. If he came from one of the tribal cultures, such as the Gola, which has an individualistic and somewhat capitalistic orientation, he might play the game of exploitation in the same way as his Americo-Liberian counterpart. Until family, tribal, or regional affiliations develop as social restraining mechanisms in the politics of the interior, the exploitation of the uneducated tribal masses by their young evolved kinsmen may in the immediate future be even more relentless than the exploitation of the past.

A similar process but with sharply differing effects occurs in the network of government schools which are steadily reaching some of the remote areas of the Republic. The assignment of teachers to Monrovia and other coastal school systems is made strictly on a political basis, with the teachers from the leading families having prior claims. Being in Monrovia, they can frequently hold down a second job, which permits them to compensate for their low teaching salaries. The teacher posted upcountry tends to be less dedicated to the existing order of privilege than his coastal counterpart. Covertly, and even overtly, the teacher in the hinterland becomes an advocate of a more rapid change in the political, economic, and social system. Experiencing fewer of the rewards of modernization, despite his significant investment in time, he resents and opposes the many involuntary salary deductions for the True Whig Party and other projects. He tends, too, to resent the unpredictable intrusions into his professional affairs by politicians and private Americo-Liberians alike. Feeling cheated by the social system, the teacher in the interior cannot avoid conveying his sense of frustration to his students.

Furthermore, the ruling elite's disdain of commerce and industry may be their undoing. Given the present scale of economic growth and the discovery of new deposits of iron ore, it may be possible for some time to continue the un-economic use of foreign personnel to manage the burgeoning economy. At a certain point, however, higher wages, housing, and other perquisites make the recruitment of non-Liberian personnel a costly enterprise. Coupled with this development is the fact that the expanding scholarship programs for higher education have already created a pool of talent that the regime simply cannot absorb en masse into governmental sinecures and yet cannot permit to become part of an unemployed intellectual group, clustering in Monrovia and other urban communities. Hence, it seems inevitable that the educated tribal youth will eventually be displacing the foreign managerial personnel. It is doubtful whether this group would long remain content with the slow pace of change of the 1960's.

It is unlikely, too, that the migrant worker will long continue to be satisfied with the unskilled or semiskilled jobs currently offered him when he leaves the security of his tribal area. So rapid is the pace of change that by 1968 approximately one-third of the tribal people were involved in some phase of the money economy. As the migratory laborers travel from place to place, the mixed message of despair and hope becomes ever more difficult to stifle with the rhetoric of progress and free enterprise mouthed by the leaders of society. Returning to his rural homeland, the migrant, who has seen the life that prosperity has brought to other Liberians, finds it more and more difficult to accept the mounting taxes, the extortions from itinerant soldiers, and the illegal demands for labor made by officials and private Americo-Liberians alike. Indeed, the level of agitation was bound to be raised by such acts as the revolutionary step LAMCO took in 1967 of agreeing to pay its mechanics as high as $1.20 an *hour*—twice what Firestone and Liberian rubber growers were paying unskilled laborers per *day* just a few years ago.[3]

Unorganized discontent among the masses, however, has never been a sufficient factor in itself to bring about revolutionary change. Political action requires leadership, and thus far all the leadership talent has been monopolized, seduced, or suppressed by the Americo-Liberian class. The disaffected peasant or mine worker is not likely to find the leader for his cause among the Old Guard of the settler elite, even though the latter has been a frequent critic of President Tubman. Nor at this stage can radical leadership be anticipated from the group of "new" Liberians, the young, educated, and polished officials with whom Tubman surrounds himself today. Having just eased the Old Guard from the stage, this group is now eager to enjoy its inheritance. The discontented peasant also fails to find aggressive opposition leadership from his young Western-educated kinsmen, many of whom—as noted above—are busily developing entrenched private interests in the "new politics" of the hinterland counties. At the national level, moreover, the tenure of either young or elderly officials who have too openly paraded their tribal origins has been brief, and occasionally brutal. Indeed, the tribal person who succeeds in gaining prominence on the national scene often becomes almost a caricature of Old Guard Americo-Liberian manners and mores.

[3] *Ibid.*, 27 Jan. 1968, p. 89.

The Panic Button

Whether or not the latent forces are seeking a radical change in the pace and character of development in Liberia, there are very clear signs that the regime is far from confident of its ability to exercise total control over the drama that has been unfolding during the quarter-century of Tubman's rule. There is, for example, a growing pattern of overreaction to criticism of the regime. Journalists, even those working for government newspapers, are jailed or reprimanded, teachers dismissed, and foreigners declared "PNG" (*persona non grata*) for trivial indiscretions or slights against the reputation of the President or the ruling elite. The fact that Tubman did not even go through the charade of permitting an opposition candidate to contest his election in 1963 and 1967 was taken by many as a sign of increasing fear of dissent. At the legislative level, moreover, the regime has apparently never sufficiently recovered from the scare of 1955 to permit electoral challenges to the Whig candidates for the House and Senate. Finally, the elite has dealt ruthlessly with challenges to its economic supremacy, making it impossible for a vigorous and independent labor union leadership to emerge in Liberia.

Another sign of stress is the greater frequency and the intensity of public violence. Even the President is not immune. In addition to the major attempt on his life in 1955, there have been a series of alleged plots to assassinate Tubman, such as the military crisis of 1963, when several leading officials of his government were implicated. There was also the abortive plot—or alleged plot—to overthrow Tubman's regime during his visit to Switzerland in 1966. One of the more recent manifestations of the plot syndrome came in March, 1968, with the arrest of Henry Fahnbulleh, a prominent Vai, who had been serving as Liberian ambassador to Tanzania and Kenya. The treason trial, which led to his conviction and imprisonment for twenty years at hard labor, was given shrill coverage in the Liberian press. It was alleged that Fahnbulleh had plotted in East Africa to have Chinese guerrilla-warfare experts smuggled into Liberia and had planned to infiltrate subversive agents into Monrovia's radio stations to facilitate his seizure of power. Statements by students and others during the trial constituted, in the memory of long-time observers, the first case of open criticism of the President. Indeed, students who attended the trial were warned that they were guilty of disloyalty in their cheering of the defendant and booing of the prosecution witnesses. It was apparent that the government was alarmed, even though Tubman in a press conference attempted to attribute student unrest around the world to the fact that "mothers these days have stopped breast-feeding their babies. They begin feeding babies with cow's milk as soon as they are born. Thus, they develop a cow's instinct." [4]

Violence has always been just below the surface in Li-

---

[4] Fahnbulleh was also charged with having written the Nigerian ambassador indicating that "one fine day, aborigines like our counterpart, the gallant Ibos, will rise up against their reactionary minority clique to regain their fatherland." Purportedly another letter went to the Israeli ambassador accusing the Liberian government of signing a secret agreement with the American government to deport fifty thousand Black Muslims to Liberia. The letter supposedly stated that "African states which maintain ties with your Zionist government are colonial stooges and lackeys, especially so our own Liberian government." *West Africa,* 16 March 1968, p. 324. See also *West Africa,* 6 July 1968, p. 791, and 20 July, p. 847.

berian social relations, but during the first decade or more of the Tubman era the elaborate system of surveillance as well as the system of rewards to cooperative tribal leaders kept the dissatisfied element suppressed. The expanding economy and the greater freedom of movement by tribal people seeking employment have created polyglot urban centers that have strained the population-control apparatus of the regime to its limits.[5] Observers of the Monrovia riots in September, 1961, and of the series of strikes at Firestone, LAMCO, and elsewhere in 1966 commented on how volatile the disturbed situation became in a very short time. The reaction of the government was equally swift and violent, and the police dealt ruthlessly with the strikers and their leaders. The emergency powers granted Tubman in February, 1966, were regarded by many as extraordinarily excessive, but then one must remember that the first strike occurred concurrently with the military coups in Nigeria and Ghana.[6] The point, however, is that overreaction on the part of the regime not only breeds a more serious alienation on the part of those directly in-

[5] Arnold Zeitlin, an AP writer, reported in April, 1968, that a rash of graffiti was appearing on walls in Sinkhor, the fashionable suburb of Monrovia's elite. "Shameless Dog" and other signs protest the difference in living standards of the two classes. One sign that read "Death to all Congo Bitches" illustrates the curious way in which all descendants of settlers are designated by the lowest class of that group, just as "Honky" has become the black-militant term for all whites in America in 1968.

[6] The emergency powers, which expired on 8 Feb. 1967, authorized the President to increase the National Guard, mobilize society for defense, move the seat of government, set up special monetary arrangements, establish emergency hospitals, suspend habeas corpus, forbid strikes, and take other steps necessary for dealing with any internal or external threat to the government.

volved but also raises questions of the effectiveness of Tubman's policies in capturing the support of the tribal masses. Apparently the violence and the overreaction surprised even Tubman. He proclaimed the last week of February, 1966, a national week of prayer and fasting for the safety and perpetuity of their country. Tubman called for all Liberians to gather in places of worship

with lowly and contrite hearts, garbed in sackcloth and ashes or ordinary apparel, and pray for the peace of our country . . . (the prayers are not the outcome of fear) or a result of the quickening of timorous hearts and souls, nor an outburst of excited emotions or alarms. (They are rather) an earnest desire to convict ourselves of our sins, transgressions, and wickedness—to repent of them, and seek forgiveness and blessings.[7]

In perfecting the instruments for controlling outbreaks of violence on the part of the tribal majority, moreover, there were dangers that the regime might be compelled to accelerate the professionalization of the army and the police. In the process the regime could be creating a monster that it would no longer be able to control. Thus, the True Whig Party, like other inefficient single-party regimes in Africa, might find itself dislodged from power by a more technologically oriented and disciplined military group.

It is a commentary upon the fragile character of the process of evolutionary change in Liberia that so much depends upon the future of one man, President William V. S. Tubman. It is Tubman who, during more than a quarter of a century of rule, has been the Grand Scenarist, skillfully manipulating and maneuvering and in the pro-

[7] *West Africa*, 26 Feb. 1966.

cess irreversibly altering the rules of the political game. For all of his authority, however, Tubman is not a dictator. He has served rather as the managing director of an experiment in controlled change, and he has not been able at any particular moment to stray too far from the interests of the Americo-Liberian group that constitutes his main base of political power. Nevertheless, to the possible detriment of his own program of long-range reform, he has become the Indispensable Man. Tribal challengers to his authority have not lingered long on the scene, and few Americo-Liberians have been able to build substantial bases of support among the tribal people without sacrificing their credit with the Americo-Liberian elite. The frequency of Tubman's extended health leaves and his age compel the leadership of the Liberian state to ask the long-avoided question: "After Tubman, what?"

Presidents of the Republic of Liberia

Joseph Jenkins Roberts	1848–1856
Stephen Allen Benson	1856–1864
Daniel Bashiel Warner	1864–1868
James Spriggs Payne	1868–1870
Edward James Roye [1]	1870–1871
James S. Smith [2]	1871–1872
Joseph Jenkins Roberts	1872–1876
James Spriggs Payne	1876–1878
Anthony William Gardiner [3]	1878–1883
Alfred F. Russell [4]	1883–1884
Hilary Richard Wright Johnson	1884–1892
Joseph James Cheeseman [5]	1892–1896
William David Coleman [6]	1896–1900
Garretson Wilmot Gibson [7]	1900–1904
Arthur Barclay	1904–1912
Daniel Edward Howard	1912–1920
Charles Dunbar Burgess King [8]	1920–1930
Edwin Barclay [9]	1930–1944
William Vacanarat Shadrach Tubman	1944–

[1] Deposed. [2] Succeeded Roye, accepted truncated term of office.
[3] Resigned. [4] Completed unexpired term of Gardiner.
[5] Died in office.
[6] Completed unexpired term of Cheeseman; elected in own right; forced to resign.
[7] Completed unexpired term of Coleman; elected in own right.
[8] Forced to resign. [9] Completed unexpired term of King.

Summary of
Population Census 1962

		Per cent
A. LIBERIA TOTAL	1,016,443	
B. COUNTIES AND TERRITORIES *		
Grand Bassa	99,566	9.8
Grand Cape Mount	32,190	3.2
Maryland	39,349	3.9
Montserrado	166,797	16.4
Sinoe	44,639	4.4
Kru Coast Territory	21,280	2.1
Marshall Territory	14,442	1.4
River Cess Territory	28,756	2.8
Sasstown Territory	9,540	0.9
Total Counties and Territories	456,559	44.9
C. PROVINCES *		
Central	325,230	32.0
Eastern	63,712	6.3
Western	170,942	16.8
Total Provinces	559,884	55.1
D. TRIBAL COMPOSITION		
Liberian Tribal Affiliated	969,179	
Non-Liberian Tribal Affiliated	8,845	
Liberian Non-Tribal	23,478	

* The territories and provinces have since been organized into counties.

E. FOREIGN BORN POPULATION BY CITIZENSHIP

Africa

Ghana	4,095
Guinea	4,899
Ivory Coast	1,131
Sierra Leone	4,685
Other African Countries	1,179

New World

Latin America (including Haiti)	462
United States of America	1,876

Asia, Middle East

Israel	83
India	154
Lebanon	2,077
Other Asian Countries	231

Western Europe

Italy	699
Spain	470
Netherlands	481
Sweden	383
United Kingdom	293
Federal Republic of Germany	275
Other Europeans	632
Total	31,633

Bibliographic Essay

I. *Government Documents*

Official government documents of Liberia have for the most part been either typewritten or mimeographed until very recently and have had only a limited distribution abroad. Even the regular departments in Monrovia do not have workable collections of annual reports of the respective departments. The government documents in the Department of State Archives, moreover, have been largely inaccessible to scholars. For the purposes of this study, the writer found invaluable the various annual reports to the Legislature of the following individuals and agencies: the Secretary of the Interior (now Internal Affairs), the Attorney General, the Department of State, the Civil Service Commission, the Treasury, the Department of Public Instruction (now Education), the Department of Planning and Economic Affairs, the Departments of Commerce and Agriculture (formerly combined), and the National Public Health Service. A useful listing of a wide range of documents issued by governmental agencies is contained in Svend E. Holsoe, "A Bibliography of Liberian Government Documents," *African Studies Bulletin,* 11 (April 1968), pp. 39–62, and the subsequent issue.

The Secretary of the Interior generously made available to this writer the typewritten and mimeographed copies of the "Decisions Rendered by the President of Liberia on Administrative and Other Matters Heard and Determined in His Several Councils of Chiefs." These are important to the understanding of the Tubman Unification Policy and clarify many provisions of the *Liberian Code of Laws of 1956* (Ithaca,

N.Y.: Cornell University Press, 1957) regarding the administration of the interior. Also helpful in this latter respect was the mimeographed copy of the "Revised Laws and Administrative Regulations for Governing the Hinterland, 1949," which differ in certain marked respects from the *Code* provisions.

Various publications of the Division of Statistics (formerly in the Department of Agriculture and Commerce but now within the Bureau of Economic Research) were also useful. These include the *Census of Population of Monrovia* (CP Report no. 3–1956), *Census of Population of Greenville* (CP Report no. 1–1958), *Balance of Payments for 1959* (BP Report no. 1–1960), and *Foreign Trade Supplement for 1959* (FT Report no. 1–1960). The first national census was conducted in 1962, and the results are published in the National Planning Agency's *The Structure of the Liberian Population* (M.S. El-Imam, 1962). It is remarkably comprehensive in its coverage and analysis.

Liberia Today, a quarterly bulletin of events and general information, was published by the Department of State through its embassies abroad from 1951 through 1961. The Liberian government has also sponsored the publication of two bimonthly magazines containing information on economic development, trade, and investment opportunities. *Liberia Trade, Industry and Travel,* started in 1958, and *Liberian Agriculture and Commerce,* launched in 1961, are both published by Consolidated Publications, London.

Cornell University Press has been publishing two series on behalf of the Liberian government. Both are the products of the Liberian Codification Project under the direction of Professor Milton R. Konvitz. The first is the series of *Liberian Code of Laws of 1956* (1957–58). The second is the multivolume *Liberian Law Reports* (1955–62), which contain the decisions of the Supreme Court from 1861 onward.

II. *Newspapers, Journals*

Although numerous newspapers have been published in Liberia during its history as a colony and republic, political and financial considerations usually gave them brief lives. Files are either incomplete or nonexistent with respect to many of them. A discussion of newspaper sources covering the early period is found in Charles H. Huberich, *The Political and Legislative History of Liberia* (2 vols.; New York: Central Book Co., 1947), II, 1682ff. Of Monrovia's three current newspapers, the government-owned *Liberian Age* has appeared semiweekly since 1946 and *The Star* daily since 1965. Both present a fairly broad coverage of local and national news and are available on Library of Congress microfilm. The *Daily Listener* is owned by a local political leader and has a modest government subsidy. Although its reporting and typesetting make it the butt of everyone's joke, it is an invaluable source of local social items.

Two scholarly journals produced by scholars in Liberia have appeared and hopefully will not suffer the fate of other such ventures. *The Liberian Historical Review,* launched in 1966, contains useful articles by Liberian and foreign scholars as well as tracts by Liberian officials. *The Liberian Law Journal* was started in 1965, and also attempts to combine scholarly efforts with official expositions on legal subjects. A third periodical, *Liberian Studies Journal,* was started at DePauw University (Greencastle, Ind.) in 1968.

III. *Books, Articles, and Pamphlets*

A. HISTORICAL BACKGROUND

There is no single work which can be regarded as the definitive history of Liberia. Much of the story can be pieced together from the several scholarly studies which have the defect, unfortunately, of either being concerned with one narrow segment of Liberia's history or being compendium-like in approach. A great deal of the vital history of the Republic can be obtained only from an exhaustive search of accounts by missionaries, diplomats, merchants, and other observers who were not concerned with the critical separation of fact from fancy or who had a vested interest in altering some aspect of Liberian life.

Among the outstanding scholarly contributions to historical studies of Liberia is the two-volume work by Huberich, cited above, which brings together some of the most significant documents of the pre-1847 period and contains interesting biographical sketches of the pioneers. Aside from its almost exclusive concern with the colonial period, its main limitations is its formal legalistic approach to so exciting a topic. Among the better specialized treatments of the background of the American Colonization Society and the early settlers are P. J. Staudenraus, *The African Colonization Movement, 1816–1865* (New York: Columbia Univ. Press, 1961) and a mimeographed paper by Wolfe W. Schmokel, "Settlers and Tribes: The Origins of the Liberian Dilemma" (c. 1965). General studies which deal with Liberian history (and contain contradictory statements of fact) are Frederick A. Durham, *The Lone-Star of Liberia* (London: E. Stock, 1892); Sir Harry Johnston, *Liberia* (2 vols.; London: Hutchinson, 1906), vol. I; Frederick Starr, *Liberia* (Chicago, 1913); Reginald C. F. Maugham, *The Republic of Liberia* (New York: Charles Scribner's, 1920); Henry F. Reeve, *The Black Republic* (London: H. F. and G. Witherby, 1923); Raymond L. Buell, *The Native Problem in Africa* (2 vols.; New York: Macmillan, 1928), II, 704–890. The Johnston volume, despite its innuendo, is particularly good on the nineteenth-century republican period. Starr's primary asset is his analysis of the early twentieth-century political behavior of the Liberians, which reveals the historical depth of current practices. More superficial but nonetheless informative on the first two decades of the present century are the Reeve and Maugham studies. The work by Buell constitutes one of the best, albeit brief, treatments of the period from the founding of the settlements to the establishment of the Firestone Plantations Company in the 1920's. A more general study of Liberia is Hilton A. Phillips, *Liberia's Place in Africa's Sun* (New York: Hobson Press, 1946), which is largely an uncritical hymn of praise to Liberia. Its flattering tone is surpassed only by Lawrence Marinelli's *The New Liberia* (New York: Praeger, 1964). At the opposite extreme is Arthur I. Hayman and Harold Pearce, *Lighting Up Liberia* (New York: Creative Age Press, 1943), which is caustic in its analysis. Finally, for historic purposes, reference should be made to J. Büttkofer, *Reisebilder aus Liberia* (Leiden: E. J. Brill, 1890), which is a description of geographic and ethnographic expeditions to Liberia in 1879–1882 and 1886–1887.

Liberian scholars themselves have attempted to reconstruct their history. Two recent efforts include the doctoral dissertation of Hannah A. Bowen Jones, "The Struggle for Political and Cultural Unification in Liberia, 1847–1930" (Evanston: Northwestern Univ., 1962); and *Liberia's Past and Present* (London: Diplomatic Press, 1959) by Nathaniel R. Richardson, the Liberian government printer. Although the latter is a strange mélange of the significant as well as the inconsequential, and of historical fact as well as rumor, it is still a very useful compendium of historic speeches, treaties, and biography. One of the earliest studies by a Liberian is Thomas McCants Stewart, *Liberia, the Americo-African Republic* (New York: E. O. Jenkins, 1886). One of the most frequently cited works is Abayomi Karnga, *History of Liberia* (Liverpool: D. H. Tyte, 1962), which makes some original contribution but borrows heavily from the works of Johnston and other scholars. Two textbooks by Liberian political leaders for use in civics courses have appeared in recent years: Ernest J. Yancy, *Historical Lights of Liberia's Yesterday and Today* (rev. ed.; New York: Jaffee, 1954), and Richard and Doris Henries, *Liberia, the West African Republic* (New York: Jaffee, 1958). In terms

of understanding the process of political socialization and
Tubman's Unification Policy, they are often highly informative for what they do not say, as well as what they do. The
Yancy and Henries volumes have served as required civics
books in the Liberian schools, despite the fact that almost no
attention is given to the contribution made by tribal people to
modern Liberia, and certain historic events are glossed over or
omitted entirely. Yancy's father was Vice-President at the time
of the League of Nations investigation of slavery.

Apart from the general studies, certain works are useful for
the understanding of particular periods and events in Liberian history. The character of the colonial period, for example, is well revealed in Jehudi Ashmun, *History of the
American Colony of Liberia from December 1821 to 1823*
(Washington, D.C.: Day and Gideon, 1826); *Ralph R. Gurley,
Life of Jehudi Ashmun, Late Colonial Agent in Liberia*
(Washington, D.C.: J. C. Dunn, 1835); William Innes, *Liberia* (Edinburgh: Waugh and Innes, 1831) ; Archibald Alexander, *A History of Colonization on the Western Coast of
Africa* (Philadelphia: W. S. Martien, 1846) ; J. H. T. McPher-
son, "History of Liberia," *Johns Hopkins University Studies
in Historical and Political Science,* 9th ser. (1891) , 479–540;
and Charles I. Foster, "The Colonization of Free Negroes in
Liberia, 1816–1835," *Journal of Negro History,* XXXVIII
(Jan., 1953), 41–67.

Accounts of Liberian exploration of the hinterland are not
very numerous. One classic, however, is Benjamin Anderson,
*Narrative of a Journey to Musardu, the Capital of the West-
ern Mandingoes* (New York: S. W. Green, 1870) , which
should rank with the accounts of Stanley, Speke, and other
great explorers. Two other Liberians, Seymour and Ash, penetrated the northeastern sector of Liberia and are referred to in
the Royal Geographical Society, *Proceedings,* IV, no. 4 (1860) ,
184.

The conflicts between the Americo-Liberians and Great

Britain and France over control of the hinterland are well documented in Johnston, already cited, and in the other general studies. A significant summary is contained in President Taft's message to the Senate regarding the United States Commission to Liberia of 1909: "Affairs in Liberia," U.S. Senate, 61st Cong., 2nd sess., Document no. 457 (March 25, 1910).

The controversy with the League of Nations produced a great deal of polemical literature regarding Liberia. Among the more dispassionate coverages of the subject are Raymond L. Buell, "Liberia: A Century of Survival, 1847–1947," *African Handbooks,* no. 7 (Philadelphia: University of Pennsylvania Press, 1947) and an unpublished manuscript by Wolfe W. Schmokel, "Reform and Rubber: The United States and the Crisis of Liberian Independence, 1929–1934," (April, 1963; University of Vermont). Relevant League of Nations documents include *Report by the International Commission of Inquiry into the Existence of Slavery and Forced Labor in the Republic of Liberia* (Geneva, Dec. 15, 1930; c.658.m.272.-1930.VI) ; the monthly *Official Journal,* 1929–1936; and *Annual Report of the Sixth Committee (Slavery) of the Assembly to the Council,* 1929–1936. Official American reactions are chronicled in *Foreign Relations of the United States,* 1929–1936, and Department of State, *Documents Relating to the Plan of Assistance Proposed by the League of Nations* (Washington, D.C.: Superintendent of Documents, 1933) . The British reaction is revealed in the British Blue Book, *Papers concerning Affairs in Liberia, December 1930 to May 1934* (London: His Majesty's Stationery Office, 1934), Cmd. 4614. The reaction of an African political leader who served as the first President of Nigeria until the 1966 coup is contained in Nnamdi Azikiwe, *Liberia in World Politics* (London: A. H. Stockwell, 1934) .

The outlines of President Tubman's Open-Door and Unification policies are revealed in Reginald E. Townsend, ed., *President Tubman of Liberia Speaks* (London: Consolidated

Publications, 1959), and in Republic of Liberia, Bureau of Information, *The National Unification Program of Liberia* (Monrovia: Department of State, 1954). A view of the progress of Tubman's policies from within the official family is contained in Robert A. Smith's *The Emancipation of the Hinterland* (Monrovia: The Star Magazine and Advertising Service, 1964).

B. LAND AND PEOPLE

Descriptions of the geography, economy, and society of Liberia are found in the general historical works cited above. Two postwar volumes that attempt to provide a dispassionate and readable coverage of background material are R. E. Anderson, *Liberia, America's African Friend* (Chapel Hill: University of North Carolina, 1952), and Charles Morrow Wilson, *Liberia* (New York: William Sloan Associates, 1947). A useful compendium of facts about the economy, government, history, and leading Liberian personalities is the *Liberian Yearbook, 1956* (London: Diplomatic Publishing Co., 1956), edited by Henry B. Cole, who published a revised version in 1962. Also useful is the Liberian Information Service pamphlet, *Liberia: Story of Progress* (London: Consolidated Publications, 1960).

The most significant of the earlier accounts of the economic progress of Liberia from the 1820's to World War II is George W. Brown, *The Economic History of Liberia* (Washington, D.C.: Associated Publishers, 1941). It is especially valuable for its analysis of Americo-Liberian economic attitudes, of tribal economics, and of the history of the series of disastrous foreign loans. A severe indictment of the present regime's failure to grapple with the difficult problems of institutional change and distributive justice is contained in Robert W. Clower, George Dalton, Mitchell Harwitz, and A. A. Walters, *Growth Without Development: An Economic Survey of Liberia* (Evanston: Northwestern University Press, 1966). This is the product of two years' work in Liberia by a group of Northwestern economists and other scholars, and carefully reviews all phases of the Liberian economy. Its publication was delayed by the Liberian and American governments. An abbreviated version of the work is contained in George Dalton, "History, Politics and Economic Development in Liberia," *Journal of Economic History*, Vol. 25 (1965), 569–591. Other brief articles on economics, written by Harry W. Yaidoo of the Bureau of Economic Research, appeared in *Liberia Trade, Industry and Travel*, nos. 4–8 (1959–1960). Two theses on Liberian financial problems are Nathaniel Ejiogu Kevin's M.B.A. thesis on "Financial Treaties and Foreign Investment in Liberia" (New York University, 1957) and the former Secretary of the Treasury, Charles D. Sherman's "The Effects of Foreign Loans and Concessions in Liberia," (School of Public Affairs, American University, 1947). A very interesting treatment of the Firestone loan of 1927 is contained in Frank Chalk, "The Anatomy of an Investment: Firestone's 1927 Loan to Liberia," *Canadian Journal of African Studies*, I (Mar., 1967), pp. 12–32.

The United States government, in connection with its overseas operations, has produced two documents that assess the agricultural and forestry potential of Liberia: C. R. Orton, *Agriculture in Liberia* (Washington, D.C.: Foreign Operations Administration and Department of Agriculture, 1954), and T. Holsoe, *Forest Progress and Timbering Opportunities in the Republic of Liberia* (Washington, D.C.: International Cooperation Administration, 1955). The Firestone Plantations Company has not been without its vociferous champions and critics. Perhaps the most reasonably objective study of the company's activities is Wayne Chatfield Taylor, "The Firestone Operations in Liberia," *United States Business Performance Abroad*, Case Study no. 5 (New York: National Planning Association, 1956).

The racial and class divisions within Liberia are dealt with by Johnston, Karnga, and other historians. Two scholarly appraisals of the Americo-Liberians that largely avoid adverse conclusions are Richard P. Strong, ed. of Harvard African Expedition of 1926–1927, *The African Republic of Liberia and the Belgian Congo* (2 vols.; Cambridge, Mass.: Harvard University Press, 1930), and D. F. McCall, "Liberia: An Appraisal," *Annals of the American Academy of Political and Social Sciences,* 306 (July, 1956), 88–97. Of quite another character is the highly critical evaluation of Liberian manners, morals, and politics contained in Elizabeth D. Furbay, *Top Hats and Tom-Toms* (Chicago: Ziff Davis Publishing Co., 1943), which has been banned in Liberia. Most revealing of all, perhaps, is the self-analysis conducted by some of Liberia's leading political, social, and religious leaders and set forth in John P. Mitchell, ed., of United Christian Fellowship Conference of Liberia, *Changing Liberia: A Challenge to the Christian* (Switzerland, 1959). In addition to the work by Smith on the hinterland, cited above, a very useful work on the cleavages within the social structure of Monrovia and the problems of tribal mobility are contained in the very excellent volume by Merran Fraenkel, *Tribe and Class in Monrovia* (Oxford: International African Institute, 1964). Equally useful is her shorter piece, "Social Change on the Kru Coast of Liberia," *Africa,* 36 (1966), 154–172.

Ethnographic material on Liberia's tribal societies is only recently being expanded. Perhaps the most outstanding of the earlier students of Liberian tribal organization was George W. Harley, whose "Notes on the Poro in Liberia," *Papers of the Peabody Museum,* XIX (1941) and "Masks as Agents of Social Control in Northeast Liberia," *ibid.,* XXXII, no. 2 (1950), are essential reading for the understanding of tribal politics. Additional material by Harley appears in George Schwab, "Tribes of the Liberian Hinterland," *ibid.,* XXXI (1947). A number of impressive Ph. D. theses by American and other students of anthropology are beginning to provide new insight into the nature of traditional tribal society in Liberia and the

234234

variety of responses to social, economic, and political change. Among the more outstanding are James L. Gibbs' "Some Judicial Implications of Marital Instability among the Kpelle" (Harvard University, 1960); Warren L. d'Azevedo's "Continuity and Integration in Gola Society" (Northwestern University, 1962); and Svend Holsoe's "The Cassava-Leaf People: An Ethnohistorical Study of the Vai People with a Particular Emphasis on the Tewo Chiefdom" (Boston University, 1967). Shorter ethnographic studies on particular tribal groups or groupings by these and other scholars include: H. Boakai Freeman, "The Vai and their Kinsfolk," *Negro History Bulletin*, XVI (1952), 51–63; James L. Gibbs, "The Kpelle of Liberia," in Gibbs, ed., *Peoples of Africa* (New York: Holt, Rinehart and Winston, 1965), 197–240; William E. Welmers, "Secret Medicines, Magic, and Rites of the Kpelle Tribe in Liberia," *Southwestern Journal of Anthropology*, V (1949), 208–243; Denis Paulme's *Les Gens du Riz: Kissi de Haute-Guinée Française* (Paris: Librairie Plon, 1954); Warren d'Azevedo, "Uses of the Past in Gola Discourse," *Journal of African History*, III (1962), 11–34; and Svend Holsoe, "The Condo Confederation in Western Liberia," *The Liberian Historical Review*, 3 (1966), 1–28. The Bureau of Folkways of the Liberian Department of the Interior has issued a series of tribal studies compiled by students of anthropology. Despite the Americo-Liberian social bias there is much information in *Tribes of the Western Province and the Denwoin People* (1955); *Traditional History, Customary Laws, Mores, Folkways and Legends of the Vai Tribe* (1954); and *Traditional History and Folklore of the Glebo* [Grebo] *Tribe* (1957). No author is indicated. Finally, reference should be made to the works of an economist, David Blanchard, on the Mano, and of an historian, Ronald Davis, on the people of the Kru Coast. Both were completing doctoral dissertations at Indiana University in 1968.

The formal structure of government is set forth in the Liberian Information Service, *Liberia: Story of Progress* (London: Consolidated Publications, 1960), and a copy of the constitution with amendments is found in the civics books by Henries and Yancy, already cited. The origins of political controversy and the emergence of political parties in Liberia as a whole and Maryland County in particular are traced in Huberich; Starr; and S. W. Laughon, "Administrative Problems in Maryland in Liberia, 1836–1851," *Journal of Negro History*, XXVI (July, 1941), 325–365.

Biographical sketches of the chief executives of Liberia are fairly numerous although not always informative. Typical of the genre is Thomas H. B. Walker, *The Presidents of Liberia* (Jacksonville, Fla.: Mintz Printing Co., 1915), intended for civics courses. Richardson, cited earlier, is much more useful despite apparent contradictions in facts. The latter volume also contains verbatim accounts of several inaugural addresses. Other presidential messages are listed in the Howard University Library, *Catalogue of the African Collection in the Moorland Foundation* (Washington, D.C.: Howard University Press, 1958). Although to Graham Greene the line between fact and fiction is very thin, an interesting treatment of his meeting with former President Edwin Barclay is presented in the classic *Journey without Maps* (London: William Heinemann, 1936).

Profiles of President Tubman are seldom neutral. Eulogies are found in Thomas P. Melady, *Profiles of African Leaders* (New York: Macmillan, 1961), and in *Liberia's Eighteenth President* (Monrovia, 1946) by Tubman's late cousin, J. Emery Knight. A more objective treatment is the sketch in David Williams, "Profile of a President," *Best Articles and Stories*, IV (April, 1960), 50–53, which was reprinted from *Africa South*. Tubman's philosophy may be extracted in part from the collection of his speeches by Townsend, cited earlier. One phase of Tubman's administration, the assassination attempt of 1955, is covered in the Liberian Information Service, *The Plot That Failed* (London: Consolidated Publications, 1959). A recent official "portrait" is contained in Robert A. Smith's *William V. S. Tubman: An Informal Study of an African Statesman* (Monrovia: Providence Publication, 1966).

The voice of the opposition to Tubman is partially expressed in a rather pitiful article by the 1951 unsuccessful presidential candidate, Dihdwo Twe, "Liberia: An American Responsibility," *Annals of the American Academy of Political and Social Science,* 282 (July, 1952), 104–107. More interesting are the soul-pricking tracts produced by Liberia's foremost "controversial figure in the community and a pamphleteer," Albert Porte. Mr. Porte's writings include "Glimpses of Justice in Liberia," "Our Constitutional Rights," "A Few Articles Refused Publication by our Newspapers," and "A Little Child Shall Lead Them—A Tribute to Maryland County." Mr. Porte is frequently jailed or cited in contempt of the Legislature.

The role of churches and other voluntary associations in Liberian social and political life is set forth in the United Christian Fellowship Conference report edited by Mitchell. The significance of the Roman Catholic Church is dealt with at length in Martin J. Bane, *The Catholic Story of Liberia* (New York: D. X. McMullen, 1950). Much of the material on relationships between family and politics has been extracted from the social notices in the *Daily Listener.*

The problems of administration within Liberia can be discerned from an examination of the annual reports of the heads of departments, which are remarkably frank in their self-criticism. A scholarly monograph dealing with the problems of administration in Grand Bassa County is J. Genevray, *Eléments d'une Monographie d'une Division Administrative Liberieenne* (Dakar: IFAN, 1952). A lighter but nonetheless informative treatment is the sketch of hinterland administration in Gbarnga District in "Our Far-flung Correspondents: Tubman Bids Us Toil," *New Yorker,* XXXIII (Jan. 11, 1958), 72–91.

For historical purposes, Abayomi Karnga, *A Guide to Our Criminal and Civil Procedure* (Liverpool: D. E. Tyte, 1926), is useful as a general outline of the Liberian legal system. One of the more damning critiques of the Liberian judiciary was delivered at the Lagos Conference of African Jurists in 1961 by C. A. Cassell, a former Attorney General under Tubman. The *Liberian Law Journal,* which was launched in 1965, contains a number of interesting articles on the problem of crime and the legal system of Liberia.

Although their works were not yet published in 1968, it might be useful to refer to the political field studies of Richard Fulton of Case Western Reserve University, who worked among the Kpelle; Martin Lowenkopf of the Hoover Institution, Stanford University, who has studied national political development; and Ronald Kurtz of Grinnell College, who has done a study of political change and modernization in a mixed tribal community.

D. CONTEMPORARY ISSUES

The role of the American missionaries and philanthropists in the development of the Liberian educational system is revealed in each of the general studies cited earlier. One detailed study of the colonial period from this point of view is Charles A. Earp, "The Role of Education in the Maryland Colonization Movement," *Journal of Negro History,* XXVI (July, 1941), 325–365. Two surveys of educational endeavors during Liberia's first century as a colony and republic are Thomas Jesse Jones, *Education in Africa* (New York: Phelps-Stokes Fund, 1922), and Allen W. Gardner, *The Trustees of Donations for Education in Liberia: A Story of Philanthropic Endeavor, 1850–1923* (Boston: Thomas Todd,

1923). The impact of education upon both tribal and settler cultures was analyzed during the period between the two world wars in James L. Sibley, *Liberia—Old and New* (Garden City, N.Y.: Doubleday, Doran, 1928), and in the postwar period by Thomas Hodgkin, "Education and Social Change in Liberia," *West Africa*, nos. 1907–1911 (Sept. 12–Oct. 10, 1953). An interesting analysis of the problems of vocational training is contained in Alvin I. Thomas' *Technical Education in Liberia* (Columbus: Epsilon Pi Tau, 1961). A more comprehensive coverage of the educational needs of Liberia in terms of its internal and external commitments was prepared for Education and World Affairs of New York in 1965, by the Study Committee on Manpower Needs and Educational Capabilities in Africa. Its fifth report deals with *Liberia: Study of Manpower Needs, Educational Capabilities and Overseas Study.*

The problems of higher education are dealt with in a straightforward manner in two works, one a Ph. D. thesis by a Liberian student, now dean of administration at the University of Liberia, and the second a report by two Americans. The first is Advertus A. Hoff, "Higher Education for a Changing Liberia" (Columbia University, 1959). The second is A. Gordon Nelson and Charles C. Hughes, *University of Liberia: An Appraisal and Recommendations with Observations and Recommendations Relative to Agriculture and Forestry* (hectograph report; Ithaca, N.Y.: Cornell University, 1960).

The foreign relations of Liberia are chronicled in many works, but it is worth while to single out three of the volumes previously cited: the two by Johnston and Azikiwe and U.S. Senate Document no. 457, "Affairs in Liberia." Two more recent treatments of Liberian-American relations are found in J. H. Mower, "The Republic of Liberia," *Journal of Negro History*, XXXII (July, 1947), 256–306, and Raymond Bixler, *The Foreign Policy of the United States in Liberia* (New York: Pageant Press, 1957). A Liberian interpretation of

United States policy with respect to his country is presented in the Ph. D. thesis of the former Secretary of Education, John P. Mitchell: "America's Liberian Policy" (University of Chicago, 1955). A French view that places Liberia more firmly in the category of an American dependency is Pierre and Renée Gosset, *L'Afrique, les Africains* (2 vols.; Paris, 1958), vol. II. A case study dealing with the general posture of the Liberian government toward Pan-Africanism is contained in my article: "Which Road to Pan-African Unity? The Sanniquellie Conference, 1959," in Gwendolen M. Carter, ed., *Politics in Africa: 7 Cases* (New York: Harcourt, Brace and World, 1966), 1–32. Finally, much insight into Liberia's role in world politics is gained through an examination of the records of the League of Nations and the United Nations. During 1961–62, Liberia was a member of the Security Council, and has long been active in WHO, ILO, UNESCO, and other specialized agencies.

IV. *Bibliographies*

Despite certain lacunae and the manner of presentation, a useful working bibliography is contained in Marvin D. Solomon and Warren L. d'Azevedo's "A General Bibliography of the Republic of Liberia," *Northwestern University Working Papers in Social Sciences,* no. 1 (Evanston: 1962). The monumental work in this regard is still in preparation by Svend Holsoe. In the meantime it is useful to consult his "A Study Guide for Liberia," which was published by the Development Program of the African Studies Center, Boston University (1967).

Index